Get Ready! for Social Studies
GOVERNMENT AND CITIZENSHIP

Books in the *Get Ready! for Social Studies* Series:

Essays, Book Reports, and Research Papers
Geography
Government and Citizenship
U.S. History
World History

Nancy White and Francine Weinberg, series editors, have been involved in educating elementary and secondary students for more than thirty years. They have had experience in the classroom as well as on dozens of books and electronic projects. They welcome this partnership with parents and other adults to promote knowledge, skills, and critical thinking.

Get Ready! for Social Studies
GOVERNMENT AND CITIZENSHIP

David Pence, Jr.

Series Editors
Nancy White
Francine Weinberg

McGraw-Hill
New York   Chicago   San Francisco
Lisbon   London   Madrid   Mexico City
Milan   New Delhi   San Juan   Seoul
Singapore   Sydney   Toronto

Library of Congress Cataloging-in-Publication Data applied for.

McGraw-Hill

A Division of The *McGraw-Hill* Companies

1 2 3 4 5 6 7 8 9 0   QPD/QPD   0 9 8 7 6 5 4 3 2

ISBN 0-07-137760-3

This book was set in Goudy Oldstyle by North Market Street Graphics.

Printed and bound by Quebecor/Dubuque.

McGraw-Hill books are available at special quantity discounts to use as premiums and sales promotions, or for use in corporate training programs. For more information, please write to the Director of Special Sales, Professional Publishing, McGraw-Hill, Two Penn Plaza, New York, NY 10121-2298. Or contact your local bookstore.

 This book is printed on recycled, acid-free paper containing a minimum of 50% recycled, de-inked fiber.

Contents

Introduction

In recent years, the media have told us that many students need to know more about history, geography, and civics and to improve their writing skills. While schools are attempting to raise standards, learning need not be limited to the classroom. Parents and other concerned adults can help students too. *Get Ready! for Social Studies* provides you with the information and resources you need to help students with homework, projects, and tests and to create a general excitement about learning.

You may choose to use this book in several different ways, depending on your child's strengths and preferences. You might read passages aloud, you might read it to yourself and then paraphrase it for your child, or you might ask your child to read the material along with you or on his or her own. To help you use this book successfully, brief boldface paragraphs, addressed to you, the adult, appear from time to time.

Here is a preview of the features you will find in each chapter:

Word Power

To help students expand their vocabulary, the "Word Power" feature in each chapter defines underlined words with which students may be unfamiliar. These are words that students may use in a variety of contexts in their writing and speaking. In addition, proper nouns and more technical terms appear in boldface type within the chapter, along with their definitions. For example, the word decade is defined as "period of ten years" on a "Word Power" list. The word **cartography** would appear in boldface type within the chapter and be defined there as "the science of mapmaking."

What Your Child Needs to Know

This section provides key facts and concepts in a conversational, informal style to make the content accessible and engaging for all readers.

Implications

This section goes beyond the facts and concepts. Here, we provide the answers to students' centuries-old questions, "Why does this matter?" and "Why is this important for me to know?"

Fact Checker

A puzzle, game, or other short-answer activity checks children's grasp of facts—people, places, things, dates, and other details.

The Big Questions

These questions encourage students to think reflectively and critically in order to form a broader understanding of the material.

Skills Practice

Activities provide the opportunity for children to learn and to apply reading, writing, and thinking skills basic to social studies and other subjects as well. These skills include learning from historical documents, map reading, identifying cause and effect, comparing and contrasting, and writing analytically and creatively.

Top of the Class

In this section, creative suggestions help students stand out in class. By taking some of these suggestions, students can show their teachers that they have been putting in the extra effort that means the difference between average and excellent performance.

The book you are now holding in your hand is a powerful tool. It will help you boost your child's performance in school, increase his or her self-confidence, and open the door to a successful future as a well-educated adult.

Nancy White and Francine Weinberg

CHAPTER 1

Foundations of United States Government

This flowchart provides an overview of how each of the three branches of the U.S. government checks and balances the other two branches.

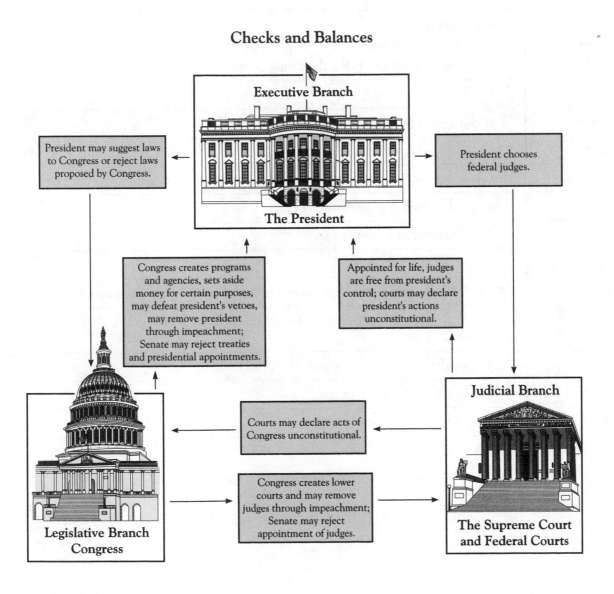

Checks and Balances

Executive Branch

The President

President may suggest laws to Congress or reject laws proposed by Congress.

President chooses federal judges.

Congress creates programs and agencies, sets aside money for certain purposes, may defeat president's vetoes, may remove president through impeachment; Senate may reject treaties and presidential appointments.

Appointed for life, judges are free from president's control; courts may declare president's actions unconstitutional.

Judicial Branch

Courts may declare acts of Congress unconstitutional.

Congress creates lower courts and may remove judges through impeachment; Senate may reject appointment of judges.

Legislative Branch
Congress

The Supreme Court
and Federal Courts

Word Power

The words on the following chart are underscored in the section called "What Your Child Needs to Know." Explain their meanings to your child as needed when they come up in reading or discussion. Keep the list handy for you and your child to use.

Word	Definition
authority	the power or right to make decisions or give orders
boundaries	borders
enforcing	making sure people obey (a law)
issued	printed (as money)
maintains	takes care of; sees to it that something is working properly
majority	more than half of a group of people
minority	less than half of a group of people
proposed	suggested in a formal way
represent	speak for (as one person *represents* a group of people in government)
society	a group of people that shares laws and cooperates for the good of its members
taxes	money the government collects from the public
violates	breaks a promise, rule, or law
void	cancel (verb); cancelled (adj.)

What Your Child Needs to Know

You may choose to use the following text in several different ways, depending on your child's strengths and preferences. You might read the passage aloud; you might read it to yourself and then paraphrase it for your child; or you might ask your child to read the material along with you or on his or her own.

WHAT IS A GOVERNMENT?

Throughout history—even in prehistoric times—human beings have been living in groups. Over time, we have learned that in order for a group to survive and succeed as a society, it needs one person or a few people to exercise authority over the members of the group. When a society is organized so that it occupies a particular place with definite boundaries and has a system for making and enforcing its own laws, the society is called a **state.** The group of people who hold authority in the state is called the **government.** This chapter reviews the basic functions of nearly all governments and examines the ideas that became building blocks for the government of the United States.

WHAT DOES A GOVERNMENT DO?

A government does more than hold authority over people. It also provides important services for them. Most governments provide the following services:

- A *government keeps order.* A government makes and enforces laws and punishes people who break them. By keeping law and order, a government helps members of a society live and work together.
- A *government provides public services.* For example, a government takes care of building roads, bridges, and tunnels. It provides transportation systems such as trains, buses, and ferries. It creates public parks. It maintains systems that bring water to people and take away waste.

- A *government protects its citizens.* A government trains and supports armed forces (an army, a navy, and an air force) to protect a state from outside invasion.
- A *government provides and controls an* **economic system.** That is, it manufactures money, collects taxes from citizens, and uses the tax money to pay for the services it provides.

THE BUILDING BLOCKS OF AMERICAN GOVERNMENT

Although governments perform many of the same functions, they differ greatly from time to time and from place to place. Following is a brief history of how the government of the United States took shape and came to be what it is today.

The English Connection

The first Europeans to settle in North America came from England. These early American colonists brought with them ideas from England—ideas that were the building blocks of our U.S. government. To understand our present government, then, we must look briefly at the history of English government.

For many centuries, England was an **absolute monarchy**—a state in which a monarch (a king or queen) has total authority over everyone. The monarch was believed to rule by **divine right**—by the will of God. The monarch's advisers were a group of nobles called the Great Council. So far, this doesn't sound anything like our government of today.

However, as early as the 1200s, things began to change. Groups in different parts of England elected people to represent them in meetings with the Great Council. Together, the Great Council and the elected representatives made up the **legislature,** or lawmaking body, of the English government. It was called **Parliament.** Later, the Great Council would be called the **House of Lords,** and the elected representatives would form the **House of Commons.**

In 1215, a group of people banded together and wrote a document called the **Magna Carta** (Great Charter). The Magna Carta said that people could not be punished, killed, or have their property taken from them by the government unless the government acted legally, or under the law. In other words, even the king could not have a person killed just because he felt like it. The Magna Carta also said that people could not be forced to pay certain taxes unless the people themselves agreed to pay them.

King John, the king of England at that time, was pressured into signing the Magna Carta. By doing so, he turned the absolute monarchy into a **limited monarchy.** There were limits set on what the monarch could do. At least in a few respects, the king had to obey the law and ask for the people's approval. The Magna Carta introduced to the world two very important ideas: the idea of **limited government**—government in which the powers of those in authority are limited by law; and the idea of **consent of the governed**—agreement by the people that they accept the authority of the state.

Much later, in 1689, the **English Bill of Rights,** was passed. This document further limited the power of the monarchy in several ways. Here are some of the ideas this important document contained: (1) monarchs do not rule by divine right; (2) the monarch must not collect taxes without the agreement of the people's representatives in Parliament; (3) the monarch cannot control elections in Parliament; (4) people accused of crimes have the right to a fair trial; (5) people convicted of crimes should not receive cruel punishments.

The rest of this chapter will show how the people who formed our government used principles that originated in England. It will also show how it was these very ideas that prompted the colonists to declare their independence from England.

Government in the Thirteen Colonies

After the signing of the Magna Carta, ideas regarding human rights and fair representation in government continued to grow and spread in England. These ideas traveled across the Atlantic Ocean when the first English colonists crossed the sea to settle in the "New World." (We call these people *colonists* because a **colony** is an area governed by a land far away—in this case, England.)

The **Virginia House of Burgesses,** a legislature made up of elected representatives, was established in 1619 in the colony of Jamestown.

Painting of *Mayflower* by Charles Austin Needham

One year later, in 1620, as the ship the *Mayflower* neared the coast of present-day Cape Cod, the people on board wrote and signed the **Mayflower Compact,** an agreement to create "just and equal laws" for the good of the colony they would form. Each person promised to obey these laws. In other words, the colony they would form would be based on consent of the governed. They founded the colony of Plimouth (now spelled *Plymouth*), in the southeastern part of what is now Massachusetts.

As the American colonies grew, England let them take care of their own affairs, for the most part. Each colony established a government, elected leaders, and set up assemblies of representatives to make laws. Each colony chose **representative democracy** as its form of government. **Democracy** means "government by the people." In a representative democracy, as opposed to a direct democracy, the people do not vote directly on specific laws; rather, the people elect representatives to vote for the laws they support. It is easy to see how the English ideas of limited government, representative democracy, and consent of the governed influenced the colonies.

Independence

After the English Bill of Rights was passed in 1689, colonists assumed that the Bill applied to them as well as to people living in England. But

Detail of painting *The Spirit of '76* by Archibald
MacNeil Willard, 1875

as time went on, colonists began to feel that they
were being deprived of the basic rights of English
people. By 1760, they thought that the king
of Great Britain, as England was then called,
was treating them unfairly. For example, **King
George III** forced colonists to pay heavy taxes for
things that everyone needed—paper, sugar, glass,
and tea.

The colonists certainly did not agree to these
taxes, and they were not allowed to send elected
representatives to bring their complaints to Parliament. This is how the expression "no taxation
without representation" became a slogan of the
colonists. Finally, when George III sent British soldiers to enforce his unfair laws in the colonies, the
colonists decided they must stand up for their
rights. They still considered themselves loyal to
Great Britain, and they wanted the rights promised
to all British people.

American political leaders such as **Samuel**

Adams and **George Washington** met in the fall of
1774 and decided to stop all trade with Britain. In
April 1775, gunfire broke out between British soldiers and colonists in Lexington, Massachusetts.
The war for independence known as the **American Revolution** had begun.

Within a few weeks, **delegates,** or representatives, from each colony met in Philadelphia. They
ordered that an army and a navy be organized and
that money be <u>issued</u> to pay for the war. The
delegates asked **Thomas Jefferson** to write a document stating that the colonies were now independent from Britain. That document, completed
and signed in 1776, is our **Declaration of Independence.**

In addition to stating that the colonists were
now separate from Great Britain, the Declaration
of Independence also stated that a new government would be formed, built on the ideas of human
liberty and consent of the governed. With the signing of the Declaration of Independence, the thirteen American colonies became the United States
of America, and the colonists began to think of
themselves as Americans.

The Articles of Confederation

When the war was over and the Americans had
won, the new country needed a permanent **federal,** or national, government to bind the thirteen states together. The delegates, however,
were afraid to take power away from the individual states and turn it over to a central government. They didn't want to go back to living
under a monarchy, and that is what they feared
might happen if they made the federal government too strong. The delegates finally agreed on
a plan for a simple federal government consisting
of a council, made up of elected representatives
from each state. The plan was called the Articles
of Confederation. The Articles allowed individual states to keep their power and independence.
In fact, they gave so much power to the states
that the federal government was left far too
weak. When states could not agree on issues
such as borders, taxes, and trade, the federal government did not have the authority it needed to
step in and make decisions.

THE CONSTITUTION

In May 1787, all thirteen states sent delegates to Philadelphia once again to take part in the **Constitutional Convention.** There, the Constitution of the United States, which would replace the Articles of Confederation, was written. It mapped out a new plan for government and clarified the new government's powers and duties. The people who participated in the creation of this important document are known as the **framers** of the Constitution. The Constitution continues to guide our nation today.

The Constitutional Convention

The fifty-five state delegates spent the summer of 1787 deciding what would be in the Constitution. During the four months the Constitutional Convention remained in session, delegates argued about how to divide power between the federal government and the governments of the individual states. They split into two groups. The **Federalists,** led by **John Adams,** supported a strong federal gov-

Constitution of the United States

America's First Constitution

More than two hundred years before the U.S. Constitution was drafted, Native American leaders in what is now New York State developed an unwritten constitution that united the **Iroquois Confederation of the Five Nations.** The Five Nations included the Cayuga, Mohawk, Oneida, Onondaga, and Seneca tribes. These tribes joined together in order to gain strength. The constitution was spoken aloud and agreed upon in 1570.

Each nation included several groups called *clans.* Each clan sent its chief to represent it at meetings of the Confederation. Therefore, the larger nations, or those with more clans, were represented by more chiefs than the smaller nations. To ensure equality among the Five Nations, each nation's group of chiefs had only one vote on Confederation issues. Clan chiefs, therefore, had to agree before casting a vote for their nation.

The Confederation's constitution clarified this organization, as well as various rules and goals. It helped the Five Nations avoid war among themselves for over two centuries. The success of the Confederation of the Five Nations impressed the leaders of the new United States of America. They saw in the Confederation an inspiring example of representative government. They used the Confederation's oral constitution as a model as they set about drafting their own Articles of Confederation in 1777.

During the American Revolution, some Confederation members supported the colonies, while others supported the British. This split finally broke up the Confederation.

ernment; the **Anti-Federalists,** led by Thomas Jefferson and **James Madison,** believed that the Constitution gave too much power to the federal government and too little to the state governments.

The delegates finally agreed on what the federal and the state governments could and could not do. For example, the Constitution says that the federal government has the power and the responsibility to maintain an army and a navy, whereas state governments control school systems and make laws about marriage and divorce. Some powers are shared by federal and state governments. For example, both have the power to tax citizens, establish courts, and make laws.

Delegates also disagreed about how many representatives the states would have in the legislature, which was called **Congress.** Should all states be represented equally? Or should states with more people have more representatives than states with fewer people? Finally, the delegates agreed that the Constitution should establish a two-part, or **bicameral,** legislature. In other words, like the British Parliament, Congress would consist of two houses. The upper house, or **Senate,** would have two representatives from each state, but the number of representatives in the lower house, or **House of Representatives,** would depend on the number of people in each state. In the House, therefore, the more heavily populated states would have more representatives.

The Main Ideas

The framers of the Constitution based their work on six main ideas:

1. **Popular sovereignty,** or rule by the people. The delegates focused on creating a limited government that would take the form of a representative democracy.
2. **Federalism.** The Constitution was based on the Articles of Confederation, which had given most of the power to the thirteen states. Now the framers saw the need for a stronger federal government.
3. **Separation of powers.** The Constitution established three branches of government and divided power among them. The **legislative** branch, which has the power to make laws, consists of the Senate and the House of Representatives; the **executive** branch, which has the power to carry out the laws, consists of the president, the vice president, and others; the **judicial** branch, which has the power to make decisions regarding laws, consists of the U.S. Supreme Court and lower federal courts. This separation was designed to prevent a single person or group from growing too powerful.

(More about each branch of our government appears later in this book.)

4. **Checks and balances.** The framers had another way to make sure that no branch of government would become too powerful: each of the three branches of government would have some control over the other two. For example, Congress makes laws, but the president can **veto,** or cancel, a law. Then Congress can cancel out the veto if two-thirds of both the Senate and the House of Representatives vote to keep the law. Another example is the right of federal courts to decide that a law passed by Congress is **unconstitutional,** or against what is written in the Constitution. But the power of the court is limited by the right of the president to choose federal judges. And that power is limited by the requirement that the Senate approve the judges appointed by the president.
5. **Judicial review.** One of the rights and duties of the courts is to decide whether any law violates the Constitution. If a law is judged to be unconstitutional, it becomes void. The Supreme Court has the right to make the final decision about any law. Not even the president can change its decisions.
6. **Limited government.** By clearly spelling out the powers the government has and does not have, the Constitution ensures that even the president's powers are not absolute, but are limited by law.

The Parts of the Constitution

For those who would like to read the U.S. Constitution, it is easy to find a copy. (The Preamble and the Bill of Rights appear at the back of this book. Try a textbook or encyclopedia or the Internet for the full text.) The following is a summary of this important document.

The Constitution is organized into three basic parts. Here are the most important ideas in each part.

The **Preamble,** or introduction, summarizes the six goals of the U.S. government: (1) to have the states work together as a single nation; (2) to treat all people fairly and equally; (3) to keep peace; (4) to protect the United States from enemies; (5) to promote the public welfare; (6) to guarantee the basic rights.

The seven **articles,** or sections, of the Constitution address several general topics. Articles I, II, and III explain the structure and roles of the legislative, executive, and judicial branches. Article IV discusses the powers of the federal government and state governments. Article V notes that, over time, the Constitution may need to be changed, and it gives guidelines on how **amendments,** or changes and additions, can be made. Article VI states that the Constitution and Congress's laws together make up the "supreme Law of the Land." The final article, Article VII, says that at least nine of the thirteen states would have to **ratify,** or approve, the Constitution before it could be formally accepted.

Article V shows that the framers thought ahead to a time when ideas or needs might change. Of course, amending the Constitution is not easy. An amendment cannot even be proposed unless two-thirds of the members of Congress agree with the change or a national convention is called for by two-thirds of the state legislatures. Later, an amendment must be ratified by three-fourths of the states.

The amendments make up the third part of the Constitution. The Constitution, with its seven articles, was ratified in 1788. Because the Anti-Federalists were afraid that the federal government would have too much power over individuals, the first ten amendments, or **Bill of Rights,** were added to the Constitution and ratified in 1791. These amendments all protect individual liberties. The First Amendment, for instance, grants people the freedom to practice any religion they choose, to speak freely, to publish their ideas and opinions in newspapers and magazines, to gather in groups, and to criticize the government.

Since the ten amendments that make up the Bill of Rights were ratified, there have been seventeen more amendments to the Constitution. Some grant individual liberties in addition to those granted by the Bill of Rights. Others cover issues from the number of times a president can be elected to the date on which a president's term of office begins, to salary raises for representatives to Congress. The most recent amendment was ratified not very long ago—in 1992. More details on the Bill of Rights and other amendments appear in Chapter 2.

HOW DOES OUR SYSTEM OF GOVERNMENT WORK TODAY?

In many ways, our system of government works today much as the framers of the Constitution planned long ago. As our country grows and changes, needs and problems arise that did not exist when the Constitution was first written. Because of the wisdom of the framers, who provided for amendments to be made, the Constitution itself can keep up with those changes. Our Constitution is, for this reason, called a **living constitution.**

The rest of this book describes and analyzes how our government works today.

! Implications

To answer the question, "Why does all this matter?" or "What does it mean?," share the following insights with your child.

- **Many Constitutional amendments focus on voting.** Many of the amendments to the Constitution concern voting rights. Why is this true? Voting is the way in which each citizen's voice reaches the government. A true representative democracy cannot exist unless every citizen is equally guaranteed the right to vote and equally protected against being denied that right. Many people take this idea one step further and say that it is not only the right but the duty of every citizen to vote.
- **The debate about the powers of the individual states and the powers of the federal government began at the Constitutional Convention.** This debate has echoed throughout our country's history. For example, the Civil War began over the question of whether states had the right to reject federal laws against slavery. States' rights were also the issue in the 1950s and 1960s when some states did not want to accept school integration as ordered by the federal government.

On the other hand, it was the Anti-Federalists at the Constitutional Convention who were responsible for the Bill of Rights. Believing that state governments would be better protectors of individual liberties than the federal government, they agreed to the Constitution only after the Bill of Rights was promised to protect individual liberties. The debate still goes on.

- **The word *democracy* comes from Greek words meaning "rule of the people." But** what happens when people in a democracy disagree about some issue? We take a vote, of course. And the <u>majority</u> rules. In other words, all citizens live by the decisions of the majority of voters, and legislators make laws according to the majority's wishes. This is how a democracy works. However, a majority with too much power could destroy the <u>minority</u>. For this reason, a democracy remains healthy only so long as the people in the majority respect the rights of the minority.

✓ Fact Checker

To check that your child knows or can find the basic facts in this chapter, here is a puzzle.

Across

2. The second part of the Constitution consists of seven _____.
3. The Magna Carta changed the absolute monarchy in England to a _____ monarchy.
5. The English Bill of Rights said that the monarch did not rule by _____ right.
6. Popular sovereignty means government by the _____.
7. The first part of the Constitution is called the _____.

Down

1. The courts determine whether or not a law is constitutional. This is called _____ review.
2. The Bill of Rights consists of the first ten _____ to the Constitution.
4. The Magna Carta introduced to England the concept of _____ of the governed.

Answers appear in the back, preceding the index.

? | *The Big Questions*

The following questions encourage your child to think critically rather than simply recall facts. If necessary, review the specific information from the preceding pages that will help your child make the necessary inferences to come up with reasonable answers.

1. What are four functions a state performs for society? Describe some of the problems that might arise if a government failed to perform these functions.
2. Explain how each of the following ideas in American government originated in England: representative democracy, a legislature with two separate divisions, limited government, consent of the governed.
3. Why were the Articles of Confederation unsuccessful? In which ways was the Constitution an improvement over the Articles of Confederation?
4. Since the Constitution was written, times and ideas have changed so much. How do you explain the fact that we still use a document that was written more than two hundred years ago to judge the fairness of our laws?

Suggested Answers

1. *A government maintains order by enforcing the law, provides public services such as transporta-* tion, protects citizens from enemy invasion by maintaining armed forces, and provides an economic system, that is, makes money and collects taxes that pay for the services the government provides. Some examples of things we would lack if a government failed to perform its functions are law enforcement, public transportation, and a military force to protect us. A government makes it possible for members of a society to live and work together in a peaceful and organized fashion. Without a government, a state cannot exist.

2. *Even before the Magna Carta was signed, representatives were elected to meet with the Great Council. The elected representatives and the Great Council formed a legislature with two divisions. The Magna Carta (1215) changed the absolute monarchy to a limited monarchy and required the consent of the governed in order for the government to collect certain taxes. The English Bill of Rights (1689) further extended the concepts of limited government and consent of the governed.*

3. *The Articles of Confederation gave too much power to the states, leaving the federal government so weak that it did not have the authority it needed to resolve disagreements among the states. The Constitution gave more power to the federal government.*

4. *Article V of the Constitution is what makes it a "living document." Providing for amendments meant that the Constitution could grow and change with times.*

Skills Practice

The following activities give your child practice in applying the skills basic to social studies. For some of the activities, your child may need to review the information in the preceding pages.

A. UNDERSTANDING CAUSE-AND-EFFECT RELATIONSHIPS

Make sure your child understands that an *effect* is something that happens as a *result* of another event—a *cause*. Have your child read the following causes and choose the correct effect for each one.

1. CAUSE: The King of England signs the Magna Carta.
   EFFECT?
   STATEMENT A: The absolute monarchy in England becomes a limited monarchy.
   STATEMENT B: The American colonies become independent.
2. CAUSE: King George III treats American colonists unfairly.
   EFFECT?
   STATEMENT A: The U.S. Constitution is ratified.
   STATEMENT B: The Revolutionary War begins.
3. CAUSE: The Anti-Federalists object that the Constitution gives too much power to the federal government.
   EFFECT?
   STATEMENT A: The Constitution is not ratified.
   STATEMENT B: Ten amendments called the Bill of Rights are added to the Constitution.

Answers
1. A; 2. B; 3. B

Evaluating Your Child's Skills: In order to complete this activity successfully, your child needs to make inferences based on facts as well as recall the facts themselves. If your child needs help, lead him or her back to the part of the chapter that covers each cause. Then show why the wrong answer choice for each question does not make sense.

B. DISTINGUISHING FACT FROM OPINION

Review with your child the definitions of the words *fact* and *opinion*. Establish that statements of fact can be checked to find out whether they are true or false, while statements of opinion are neither true nor false. Then ask your child to identify the following statements as facts or opinions. Encourage your child to explain each identification.

1. Representative democracy is the best form of government.
2. The number of representatives a state has in the House of Representatives depends on the size of a state's population.
3. Article V of the U.S. Constitution says that the Constitution can be amended.
4. The First Amendment to the Constitution is the most important amendment.
5. There are twenty-seven amendments to the Constitution.
6. Each state should have the same number of senators.

Answers
1. opinion; 2. fact; 3. fact; 4. opinion; 5. fact; 6. opinion

Evaluating Your Child's Skills: In order to complete this activity successfully, your child needs to understand the difference between fact and opinion. If your child has trouble, point out key words and phrases that are typical in statements of opinion: *best, most important, should.*

Top of the Class

Children interested in delving more deeply into the topic of this chapter can choose one or more of the following activities. They may do the activities for their own satisfaction or share what they have done in class to show that they have been seriously considering the foundations of American government.

POINTS TO PONDER

Suggest to your child that he or she raise the following issues in class.

1. What if King George had listened to and granted the colonists' demands to be treated fairly and to send representatives to Parliament? Would the colonies have remained loyal to Great Britain until this day, or would the Americans have demanded independence for other reasons? (Results of the further research project suggested next may shed light on this question.)
2. During the time when many people in the United States were protesting the Vietnam War, protesters sometimes showed their disapproval for the government's actions by burning an American flag. Recently, there has been debate about adding an amendment to the Constitution that would prohibit desecrating, or damaging, the American flag. Do you agree or disagree that such an amendment should be added to the Constitution? Whatever your opinion, what are your reasons for holding it? Raising this question in class might spark an interesting discussion.

FURTHER RESEARCH

Suggest that your child do further research to find out more about colonialism. He or she could present the findings as a written or oral report.

Find out about nations other than the United States that started out as colonies of other countries and later won independence. Examples are Spanish colonies in Latin America; French, German, British, Italian, Portuguese, and Spanish colonies in Africa; the British colonization of India; and the colonization of the Philippines by the United States. How did colonial people win independence—through peaceful means or by revolution? Colonialism was once widespread. Why are there so few colonies in the world today?

BOOKS TO READ

Suggest that your child read one or more of the following fiction or nonfiction books. Your child may want to recommend books to other students or respond to what he or she has read by offering an oral or written critique in class.

Bruchac, Joseph. *The Arrow over the Door.* Dial, 1998. Takes place during the Revolutionary War. The story is narrated by two boys—one a Quaker, one a Native American.

Goor, Ron, and Nancy Goor. *Williamsburg: Cradle of the Revolution.* Walker, 1994.

Myers, Anna. *The Keeping Room.* Walker, Atheneum, 1997. Set during the Revolutionary War. A family's home is taken over by Redcoats.

Lasky, Kathryn. *A Journey to the New World: The Diary of Remember Patience Whipple.* Scholastic, 1996. Fictional diary entries of a twelve-year-old girl. The story follows Mem on her journey aboard the *Mayflower* and during her first year in the New World.

Schleifer, Jay. *Our Declaration of Independence.* Millbrook, 1992.

CHAPTER 2
United States Citizenship

This flowchart provides a graphic explanation of how individuals proceed step by step through the process of naturalization to become citizens of the United States of America.

An Immigrant s Route to
American Citizenship

The person files a **petition,**
or application, asking to
be a citizen of the
United States of America.

The person immigrates
legally to the
United States.

The person lives in the United States
for five years in a row. If married to an
American citizen, the person needs to
live in the United States for only
three continuous years.

The person takes an oath
of allegiance to the
United States of America
and receives a certificate
of naturalization from a
federal judge.

During an investigation and a first hearing by the Immigration and
Naturalization Service, the person s background and qualifications for
citizenship are examined and tested. He or she answers questions about his
or her moral character and about American history and government.
He or she is asked to show a basic command of the English language.

Word Power

The words on the following chart are underscored in the section called "What Your Child Needs to Know." Explain their meanings to your child as needed when they come up in reading or discussion. Keep the list handy for you and your child to use.

Word	Definition
assemble	gather in a group
censorship	the removal of words or other types of expression of which a government disapproves
demonstration	an organized protest by a group of people
diplomats	people who represent their countries' governments in a foreign nation
hearing	a formal session in which people give testimony
immigrants	people who come to a new country to live there permanently
investigation	an official procedure to find out about something or someone
morality	a sense or awareness of right and wrong
persecuted	treated badly

What Your Child Needs to Know

You may choose to use the following text in several different ways, depending on your child's strengths and preferences. You might read the passage aloud; you might read it to yourself and then paraphrase it for your child; or you might ask your child to read the material along with you or on his or her own.

INTRODUCTION TO CITIZENSHIP

The Constitution protects the rights and welfare of all people in the United States. However, there are some significant differences between being a U.S. citizen and being merely a resident or visitor here. These differences are explained later in this chapter.

What exactly is a U.S. citizen? Three basic questions about citizenship are answered in this chapter:

- *How does a person become a U.S. citizen?*
- *What are the rights and freedoms an American citizen enjoys?*
- *What are a citizen's duties and responsibilities?*

THREE WAYS OF BECOMING A CITIZEN

The Law of the Soil

Like many other countries around the world, the United States of America grants citizenship to people based on a principle known as the law of the soil. A person who is born in the United States or one of its territories, such as Puerto Rico, is automatically a citizen at birth. This is the way most people become American citizens. The law of the soil grants citizenship to all children born in the United States, even if their parents are visitors from another country or <u>immigrants</u> who are not citizens. In fact, the only exceptions to the law of the soil are children born in the United States to foreign <u>diplomats</u> and children born on foreign ships traveling in American waters.

The Law of the Blood

The United States also grants automatic citizenship based on another principle called the law of the blood. This rule covers situations in which parents who are American citizens have a child in some other country. If at least one of the parents has lived in the United States for a certain amount of time, the child is automatically a citizen. The third way to become an American citizen is not automatic. Instead, a person goes through a process of **naturalization,** which means "becoming a citizen."

The Process of Naturalization

It is difficult to become a naturalized U.S. citizen. Even before applying for citizenship, an immigrant must apply for a **permanent resident visa,** a document giving the person permission to live and work in the United States permanently. There are only four ways a person can get a permanent resident visa, or "green card": by having a close relative who is a citizen or a permanent resident agree to **sponsor,** or vouch for, the person; by having an employer as a sponsor; by marrying a U.S. citizen or permanent resident; by winning the Green Card Lottery. Each year, there is a time during which immigrants can enter a lottery to win a green card. Only fifty thousand out of four hundred thousand will win. Unmarried children under eighteen years old who have a parent with a green card will be given one also. Once an immigrant has received a green card, the person must live in the United States for five years in a row, or three years if married to a U.S. citizen. After the required period of time, if the person is at least eighteen years old and has lived in the state of his or her current residence for at least three months, he or she may apply for citizenship to the U.S. Immigration and Naturalization Service (INS).

Once the application has been filed, the INS begins an <u>investigation</u> and holds a <u>hearing</u>. The investigation determines whether the person applying for citizenship arrived in the United States legally. (People who have entered illegally are generally returned to their own countries.) At the hearing, an INS official asks questions to determine whether the person is fit for citizenship. The person must show that he or she has a strong sense of <u>morality</u>; believes in democracy and supports the principles of the U.S. government; can read, write, and speak the English language; and knows some basic information about American history and American government. Most people pass the hearing.

All that remains is for the person to take the oath of citizenship before a federal judge. With this oath, the person makes the following three promises:

1. To be loyal to the American government rather than to his or her former country
2. To live according to the laws, rules, and Constitution of the United States
3. To defend the nation, and, if required, to serve in the military

After the person makes these promises, the judge gives him or her a **certificate of naturalization**— a legal document stating that the person is a U.S. citizen.

RIGHTS OF AMERICAN CITIZENS

As explained in Chapter 1, the first ten amendments to the U.S. Constitution, or the Bill of Rights, were added to the Constitution in 1791 in order to cement the liberties and rights of all American citizens. Amendments made later ensure additional rights to citizens. When a person or group of people claims that freedoms granted by these amendments are being denied by the government, the courts make rulings on whether or not the Constitution supports the claim. If a claim goes all the way to the Supreme Court, the ruling of the Supreme Court is final.

The First Amendment

The First Amendment names four basic freedoms: freedom of religion, freedom of speech, freedom of assembly, and freedom of the press. Each of the freedoms granted by the First Amendment is examined in detail as follows.

Freedom of religion means that no one will be persecuted for his or her religious beliefs. An American is free to believe—or *not* to believe— any religious idea. That is why we have **separation of church and state.** In a country where there is an official religion, the government may pressure or force people to practice that religion or deny peo-

ple the freedom to practice different religions. Even in the United States, however, religious practices that break the law are not allowed. For example, if a man's religion allows him to marry two women at the same time or if a religious ceremony calls for cruelty to animals or the use of illegal drugs, the religious practices are not allowed.

Freedom of speech means that the government cannot prevent individuals from speaking as they wish, regardless of the ideas they are expressing. The word *speech* in freedom of speech means more than just two people talking together or a person giving a speech to an audience. It also includes physical actions, such as marching or holding a peaceful demonstration. It can also mean expressing opinions through symbols and actions instead of words. The right to wear an armband or burn an American flag to protest some government action or policy is protected by the Constitution.

A few types of speech are *not* protected by the First Amendment—in fact, they are against the law. No one is allowed to give a speech that encourages people to resist the law or overthrow the government. And no one is allowed to lie about another person, in spoken words or in writing, for the purpose of harming the other person's reputation.

Freedom of assembly means that people are free to assemble in public places or in their own homes, and that their words and actions are protected by the First Amendment. It might seem odd that freedom of assembly needed to be included in the Constitution. Yet the fact is that gathering in groups is one of the first freedoms to be taken away by governments that are trying to deny freedom of expression. If the freedom to assemble is limited by a government, it might be illegal to attend a town meeting, to hold a protest demonstration, or to form or support a political party. The government does, however, put limits on this freedom in some situations. For example, demonstrations and parades usually take place in the streets, parks, or sidewalks of a community. Because of the possibility of violence during such events, the Supreme Court has ruled that police and other officials may, when necessary, limit the location and size of public demonstrations. Like symbolic speech, a demonstration by a group that wants to send a message of hatred or violence may be prohibited or restricted if the courts decide that the demonstration will cause a riot or in some other way pose a threat to public safety.

Vietnam peace demonstration, 1965

The fourth freedom granted by the First Amendment is **freedom of the press,** which, like freedom of speech, concerns the ways people use words. The term *the press* originally applied to words that were printed (by a printing *press*) and distributed to the public. Today it applies to words broadcast by radio or television or sent over the Internet, as well as words published in newspapers, magazines, or privately printed pamphlets. Freedom of the press means that people may report events and express their views in the press without government <u>censorship</u>. Even if someone criticizes the government in a newspaper article or on a TV news show, the government cannot restrict that person's freedom of expression. Nearly everybody gets information from the press every day, so freedom of the press also implies freedom for people to read or hear news and opinions that are free of censorship.

Other Amendments

Following are summaries of some other notable amendments that grant rights to individual citizens:

- The Fourth Amendment protects people from having their homes searched unless there is reasonable evidence that they are hiding something illegal (part of the Bill of Rights, ratified in 1791).
- The Sixth Amendment says that people accused of crimes cannot be punished without a fair trial (part of the Bill of Rights, ratified in 1791).
- The Seventh Amendment says that people convicted of crimes cannot be punished in cruel

and unusual ways (part of the Bill of Rights, ratified in 1791).
- The Thirteenth Amendment says that slavery is against the law (ratified in 1865).
- The Fifteenth Amendment says that no one can be kept from voting because of race or color, or because the person was once a slave. In other words, this amendment protects the right of African Americans to vote (ratified in 1870).
- The Nineteenth Amendment says that people cannot be kept from voting because of their sex; in other words, this amendment gives female citizens the right to vote (ratified in 1920).
- The Twenty-sixth Amendment gives all citizens the right to vote beginning at age eighteen (ratified in 1971).

RESPONSIBILITIES OF AMERICAN CITIZENS

Many people believe that, because of the freedoms that U.S. citizens enjoy, it is a privilege to be a citizen of the United States of America. Yet these precious rights are linked to a set of duties and responsibilities. Law requires citizens to fulfill the duties; failure to fulfill them is considered a crime. Most citizens feel they should also fulfill certain responsibilities.

One duty is simply to obey the law. A citizen convicted of a **felony,** or major crime, remains an American citizen, but, in some states, he or she loses the right to vote.

One duty no one seems to enjoy fulfilling is paying income tax, which is required by law, as stated in the Sixteenth Amendment to the Constitution. While many people complain about having to pay taxes, most adults understand that their tax money provides support for federal programs ranging from medical research to national defense, from national parks to financial assistance for people who need it. Failure to pay income tax is a crime.

Another duty of all adults who are healthy and able is to serve, from time to time, on a jury. One of the basic rights granted by the Constitution is a fair trial by jury for anyone accused of committing a crime. This right, granted by the Sixth Amendment, cannot be exercised unless each able adult citizen gives some of his or her time every few years to being a member of a jury.

At one time, most young males were required by law to serve in the army. Since 1973, serving in the military has been a choice that young men and women might make or not. Some feel that it is their responsibility to make this choice. Others prefer to fulfill their responsibilities as citizens in other ways.

While voting is one of the most treasured rights of American citizens, it a responsibility as well, although not required by law. A democracy is based on the idea that the people rule by choosing the individuals they want to govern. Yet if enough citizens in a democracy fail to make their voices heard by voting, the society will no longer reflect the choices of the people as a whole.

Good citizens find other ways, in addition to voting, to make their voices heard publicly. They write letters to newspapers or magazines about issues that concern or interest them. They support people who are running for political office by handing out leaflets, putting up posters, or contributing money to campaigns. They work together to pass or change laws. And they know that their freedom to do all these things is protected by the Constitution.

Yet another responsibility of citizens in any democracy is to become educated about the nation's laws, about the way American government works, and about the rights that every citizen possesses.

Rights and Responsibilities of Aliens

The Constitution applies not only to citizens but to anyone living in or visiting the United States. However, there are some important exceptions. **Aliens,** or noncitizens, cannot vote or serve on a jury. Like citizens, aliens have duties and responsibilities. They must pay taxes if they work or have business in the United States, and they must obey the law. All aliens, even those who have applied for U.S. citizenship, must notify the Immigration and Naturalization Service when they change their address.

! Implications

To answer the question, "Why does all this matter?" or "What does it mean?," share the following insights with your child.

- **The United States of America is primarily a nation of immigrants.** With the exception of Native Americans, the population of the United States is made up of immigrants and the descendants of immigrants—going all the way back to the English colonists who were the nation's first citizens. Awareness of this fact should help shape our attitudes toward recent immigrants to this country. It is more appropriate to view them as people continuing an American tradition than as outsiders who are different or strange.

- **Three of the four basic freedoms granted by the First Amendment protect the right to express ideas freely.** When an individual or group wants to hold a parade or demonstration in support of an idea that most people find unacceptable or offensive, people may wonder, "How can they be allowed to say those things in public?" Sometimes people have been permitted to deliver publicly even messages of hatred or racism. It is important to remember that if one person's freedom of expression can be limited, so can another's. That is why the First Amendment grants freedom of expression to everyone—not only to those whose views we agree with or approve of.

- **Granting freedom of expression invites new ideas.** By protecting a person's right to communicate his or her ideas freely, the Constitution invites people to exercise that right. Note in your local newspaper the most important issue discussed on the first page. A week later, look at the letters to the editor. If you find one or two letters expressing a particular view of that issue, you are likely to find letters expressing the opposite view as well. The fact that people know that they can express their opinions without fear of punishment or censorship provides a healthy atmosphere for new ideas to grow.

- **In reality, there are limits on any individual's freedom.** Every freedom granted to American citizens by the Constitution and its amendments is valid only so long as the exercise of those freedoms does not interfere with other citizens' rights. In short, no one is ever free to trample on the rights of others.

Fact Checker

To check that your child knows or can find the basic facts in this chapter, here is a categorizing activity that requires a grasp of the requirements, rights, and responsibilities that go along with becoming a U.S. citizen.

A U.S. citizen has certain rights and certain responsibilities. And there are certain requirements for becoming a U.S. citizen. Read the following list. Enter each item on the chart under the heading "Right," "Responsibility/Duty," or "Requirement."

sense of morality	serving on a jury	ability to speak English
freedom of speech	paying taxes	freedom of religion
belief in democracy	obeying the law	voting

Right	*Responsibility/Duty*	*Requirement*

Answers appear in the back, preceding the index.

 # *The Big Questions*

The following questions encourage your child to think critically rather than simply recall facts. If necessary, review the specific information from the preceding pages that will help your child make the necessary inferences to come up with reasonable answers.

1. At one time, it was much easier to become a naturalized U.S. citizen. Why has it become so difficult? What problems could arise if anyone could become a citizen?
2. The Constitution was ratified in 1788. Women were not permitted to vote until the Nine-

teenth Amendment was passed in 1920—more than one hundred years later. Why did it take so long for women to gain **suffrage,** or the right to vote?

Suggested Answers

1. *The arguments for limiting the number of people who may become naturalized citizens usually name the following reasons: (1) the United States could become overpopulated if too many immigrants were allowed to live here permanently; (2) perhaps there would not be enough jobs to go around, and many present U.S. citizens would become unemployed; (3) people who came from other countries might not find work themselves and would have to be supported by taxpayers' money.*
2. *Up until 1920, everyone—both men and women—simply accepted that women would not*

enjoy the same rights as men. Most people did not consider it important for women to be educated, and most assumed that women would not have the ability to make informed judgments, such as which candidate to vote for. A small but

determined group of forward-thinking women started the women's suffrage movement to fight for women's right to vote. In some ways, it can be compared with the women's movement of today.

 # Skills Practice

The following activities give your child practice in applying the skills basic to social studies. For some of the activities, your child may need to review the information in the preceding pages.

A. USING PRIMARY SOURCES

> **This activity gives your child a chance to read the original text of the important First Amendment to the Constitution. The activity also offers practice in "translating" historical documents into present-day English.**

Here is the First Amendment in the original wording, as it really appears in the U.S. Constitution. On a separate sheet of paper, rewrite the amendment in your own words so that it makes sense in modern American English.

- The seven words in italics are defined for you, following the amendment.
- The amendment is written as one long sentence. You may break it up into several shorter ones.
- You may read parts of this chapter to find any information you need to complete your "translation."

Amendment I

Congress shall make no law respecting an *establishment* of religion, or *prohibiting* the free exercise thereof; or *abridging* the freedom of speech, or of the press; or the right of the people peaceably to *assemble*, and to *petition* the Government for a *redress* of *grievances*.

establishment	making something official
prohibiting	preventing, stopping
abridging	limiting
assemble	gather in a group
petition	request, ask
redress	correction, righting a wrong
grievances	wrongdoing by the government

Suggested Answer

Congress may not make one religion the official religion of the country or stop people from practicing the religions they choose. Congress may not put limits on people's freedom of speech or freedom of the press. Congress may not stop people from holding meetings, as long as they are peaceful. Citizens are allowed to criticize the government and ask the government to correct any wrongs it has done.

> ***Evaluating Your Child's Skills:*** **In order to complete this activity successfully, your child needs to use fairly advanced language skills. A successful outcome will be a paragraph in modern American English that retains the general meaning of the First Amendment in its original version. If he or she has trouble, suggest that each semicolon be replaced with a period and a new sentence started with the words, "Congress may not . . ." Then help your child use the definitions to "translate" the text one section at a time.**

B. DEFENDING A POSITION

> **In social studies class, your child may be asked to participate in a debate. Often, students are assigned a position to defend, whether or not it is the position they agree with. This activity offers practice in thinking of ways to defend both the pro and the con sides of an issue.**

If you were participating in a debate about freedom of assembly, a right granted to citizens by the First

Amendment, you might be given the following statement and then asked to support one or the other of the two positions that follow it. Read the statement and the positions. Then give reasons to support *both* positions.

An organization that promotes racial hatred wants to hold a public demonstration. The members of the organization have agreed that the demonstration will be peaceful and none of its members' acts or words will encourage any unlawful behavior.

POSITION 1: The group should be allowed to demonstrate.

POSITION 2: The group should not be allowed to demonstrate.

Suggested Answers

POSITION 1: *The First Amendment protects the group's right to demonstrate. If the government could deny this right to one group, it could do the same to others. When we protect the freedom of expression of people we disagree with, we protect everyone's freedom of expression.*

POSITION 2: *Racist speeches and demonstrations often lead to violence, so the group's promise that the demonstration will be peaceful cannot be taken seriously.*

Evaluating Your Child's Skills: In order to complete this activity successfully, your child needs to have an understanding of the part of the First Amendment that guarantees the right of assembly. He or she must also use advanced reasoning skills. Remind your child that there are two sides to every question, so it is possible to think of reasons to back up even a position that one is against.

 # Top of the Class

Children interested in delving more deeply into the topic of this chapter can choose one or more of the following activities. They may do the activities for their own satisfaction or share what they have done in class to show that they have been seriously considering the topic of American citizenship.

A POINT TO PONDER

Suggest to your child that he or she raise the following issue in class.

Instead of beginning, "All Americans will have the right to . . . ," the First Amendment, which promises basic important rights to all U.S. citizens, begins with the words, "Congress shall make no law . . ." (see "Skills Practice A"). So the amendment really places more importance on telling the government what it *cannot* do rather than on telling citizens what they *can* do. It seems that the framers were trying to protect citizens from the government. What made them think this was necessary?

INTERVIEW

Your child might tape an interview with a naturalized citizen and share the interview in class.

If your family has a friend or relative who is a naturalized citizen, ask that person to participate in an interview about his or her experiences with gaining U.S. citizenship. With this person's permission, you might tape the interview and present it in class. Be sure to prepare your questions in advance. What you've learned about the process of naturalization from this chapter will help you think of questions. Don't ask any embarrassing questions or questions that are too personal. And always be considerate of your interviewee's feelings.

BOOKS TO READ

Suggest that your child read one or more of the following books. Your child may want to recommend books to other students or respond to what he or she has read by offering an oral or written critique in class.

Kroll, Steven. *Ellis Island: Doorway to Freedom.* Holiday House, 1995.

Mayerson, Evelyn Wilde. *The Cat Who Escaped from Steerage.* Macmillan, 1990. The story of Polish immigrants' voyage to the United States.

Ross, Lillian. *Sarah, Also Known as Hannah.* Albert Whitman, 1994. A twelve-year-old girl is sent by her Jewish mother in the Ukraine to live with her uncle in the United States.

Storm, Yale. *Quilted Landscape: Conversations with Young Immigrants.* Simon & Schuster, 1996.

CHAPTER 3
The Political Process

This chart shows how many votes each state has in a presidential election, as of the year 2000. It shows that the states with the largest populations have the most electoral votes. This chapter explains how presidents are elected by the electoral college.

Alabama 9	Georgia 13	Maryland 10	New Jersey 15	South Carolina 8
Alaska 3	Hawaii 4	Massachusetts 12	New Mexico 5	South Dakota 3
Arizona 8	Idaho 4	Michigan 18	New York 33	Tennessee 11
Arkansas 6	Illinois 22	Minnesota 10	North Carolina 14	Texas 32
California 54	Indiana 12	Mississippi 7	North Dakota 3	Utah 5
Colorado 8	Iowa 7	Missouri 11	Ohio 21	Vermont 3
Connecticut 8	Kansas 6	Montana 3	Oklahoma 8	Virginia 13
Delaware 3	Kentucky 8	Nebraska 5	Oregon 7	Washington 11
D.C. (District of Columbia) 3	Louisiana 9	Nevada 4	Pennsylvania 23	West Virginia 5
Florida 25	Maine 4	New Hampshire 4	Rhode Island 4	Wisconsin 11
				Wyoming 3

Word Power

The words on the following chart are underscored in the section called "What Your Child Needs to Know." Explain their meanings to your child as needed when they come up in reading or discussion. Keep the list handy for you and your child to use.

Word	Definition
debates	formal arguments about specific issues
discrimination	prejudice or unjust behavior
engaged	occupied
initiate	start, begin
prospective	hopeful, possible
tally	official count
volunteers	people who willingly work without getting paid

What Your Child Needs to Know

You may choose to use the following text in several different ways, depending on your child's strengths and preferences. You might read the passage aloud; you might read it to yourself and then paraphrase it for your child; or you might ask your child to read the material along with you or on his or her own.

INTRODUCTION TO THE POLITICAL PROCESS

By definition, **politics** means "activities designed to control or influence government." For example, members of the House of Representatives practice politics when they try to influence one another to support legislation that they want to pass. To win support for their causes, they may talk or write to fellow representatives, the president, or a member of the president's cabinet. Presidents practice politics by attempting to persuade Congress to pass laws that they support. And of course, **candidates**—people who are running for political office—are practicing politics when they give speeches asking people to vote for them.

But not only **politicians**—people actively <u>engaged</u> in the business of government—practice politics. All people who try to influence the government to act in ways that will be beneficial to them are practicing politics. For example, a person who writes a letter to his or her representative in Congress complaining that taxes are too high is practicing politics. A person who joins a group that wants the government to pay for cleaning up a polluted river is practicing politics as well.

In this chapter, you will learn about the importance of politics and how the political process works in the United States.

POLITICAL PARTIES

The citizens in a democracy have a right to voice their own opinions. Yet the ideas or wishes of any single citizen are likely to get lost in a country as large as the United States. If citizens form groups with others who share their views, they can put their voices together. They can even work to place their own members in positions of political power. A large group of people who share similar political views and work to put members of their group in positions of power is called a *political party*. Within a party, members may disagree on specific issues, but their general political ideas and goals are similar.

The Roots of America's Political Parties

Soon after George Washington became president in 1789, two political organizations began to take shape. They were the Federalist Party and the Democratic-Republican Party. The **Federalist Party,** led by **Alexander Hamilton,** George Washington, and John Adams, supported a strong central, or federal, government. The **Democratic-Republican Party** was led by Thomas Jefferson, James Madison, and others who believed that the United States should not be run by a strong central government. They said that individual state governments should have most of the power in running the nation.

After the 1816 presidential election, in which **James Monroe** was elected, both parties split. The part of the Democratic-Republican Party led by **Andrew Jackson** became known as the Democrats. Around 1832, the Whig Party was formed to oppose Jackson.

In 1854, when slavery was a growing issue in the United States, two groups that were against the extension of slavery to the western territories—the Northern Democrats and many of the Whigs—joined to form the Republican Party. The first Republican to be elected president was Abraham Lincoln in 1860.

In general, today's **Democrats,** like the original Federalists, believe in a strong federal government. Today's **Republicans,** like the original Democratic-Republicans, do not trust "big government." They believe that the federal government should have less power over the individual states, over business, and over individual people. Traditionally, the Democrats are thought of as supporting the "common people," while the Republicans are thought of as supporting big business and the wealthier part of the population.

Other words that are used to describe people's political leanings are *liberal* and *conservative*, and *left* and *right*. In general, **liberals** and people who lean to the **left** are Democrats, while **conservatives** and those who lean toward the **right** tend to be Republicans. But it is important to remember that there is a wide variety of opinions on individual issues within each party and within each political grouping.

A Two-Party System

There is no law setting the number of parties that can exist in the United States, but we have always had two major parties—a two-party system. In a two-party system, a pair of parties competes for political power. The leaders of each party try hard to get along with one another since they work together in various branches of federal, state, and local government throughout the year. Moreover, one party does not stay in power forever; eventually, the parties reverse roles when the party in power loses to the other party.

Third Parties in American Politics

Throughout our nation's history, third parties have participated in some elections alongside the two major parties—Democratic and Republican. A third party is any party that believes that neither major party is meeting the needs of the people and offers its own candidate to address these needs.

Third parties sprout up for various reasons. Here are three of the most common ones:

- *A party wants to draw attention to a single issue.* For example, in the years before the Civil War, the Free Soil Party was formed to protest slavery. Usually, single-issue parties do not exist for very long, since the issue in question is finally solved.
- *A party wants to make a drastic, overall change in society.* The American Communist Party, for example, is made up of people who believe that all business should be run by the government rather than by private citizens.
- *Some members of a major party break away because they do not support some of their party's ideas or their party's choice of candidates.* For example, in 2000, Ralph Nader ran for president as a member of the Green Party, organized to

focus on issues related to protection of the environment.

Though no third party has ever won a presidential election, many have affected the outcome of elections. For example, in the presidential election in 2000, some Democrats voted for the third-party candidate Ralph Nader, helping Republican George W. Bush to win the election by taking votes away from Al Gore, the Democratic candidate.

Who Makes Up a Political Party?

In the United States, while no one is required to join a political party, joining a party is very easy. Any citizen who is at least eighteen years old can register as a party member, and membership does not even obligate a person to vote for his or her party's candidate—or to vote at all. People can join either the Democratic Party or the Republican Party, or they can identify themselves as **independent** voters. One common reason for joining a party is that, in many states, only party members can vote in **primary elections**—elections in which a party chooses the candidate it will **nominate,** or choose to run, in the **general election,** or main election. (You will read more about primary elections later in this chapter.)

What Does a Political Party Do?

American political parties perform several important functions. Here are the most important ones:

- *A political party nominates candidates to run for government office.* Each party chooses the candidates who will run for offices, from that of president to that of mayor of a small town.
- *A political party educates the public about current issues and problems.* During the months before an election, a political party announces its ideas and goals for solving local or national problems. For instance, both the Democratic and the Republican parties might present the public with their views on the best way to improve education, to lower taxes, and to provide better health care for children. In this way, political parties help citizens make educated choices about the candidates for whom they will vote.
- *The party that is not in power acts as a watchdog.* The party that is in power knows that the other party will be its constant critic. This knowledge is an ever present reminder to the

party in power that it must act responsibly and listen to the will of the people.

VOTING AND ELECTIONS

Every year, the Tuesday after the first Monday in November is election day. On that day, Americans in towns and cities all over the country vote for candidates who are running for political office. The candidates may be running for the Senate or the House of Representatives, or they may be running for state or local offices. Every four years on election day, a president is chosen, in addition to other people who might be running for office. Here, we will focus on the presidential election, touching also on how senators and representatives are elected. You will read about how state and local officials are chosen in Chapters 9 ("State Government") and 10 ("Local Government") of this book.

Choosing Presidential Candidates

Politicians are very busy in the months and years before a presidential election. Those who hope to be chosen as their parties' candidates for president spend years of hard work preparing for their **campaigns.** The word *campaign* originally referred to a battle. Used with reference to an election, the word means "political battle." A political campaign includes everything a politician and his or her supporters do to persuade people to vote for that person rather than for an opponent. At first, the opponents are other people within the same party who also wish to receive the party's nomination for president. Preparations for a campaign include making plans; organizing a staff of workers; raising money; booking appearances on news programs; traveling and giving speeches; and preparing advertisements to be aired on radio or TV, printed in newspapers or magazines, or sent out in the mail. Of course, preparations also include preparing statements to let the public know where the prospective candidate stands on important issues.

Next, candidates from the two major parties are chosen state by state. Most states hold primary elections during the winter and spring months before an election. In a **closed primary,** only those registered as members of one of the major parties can vote, and they can vote only for candidates from their own party. In an **open primary,** however, anyone can vote, but only once. No one can vote in both parties' primaries. A complicated idea to understand is that when people vote in a primary election, they are not really voting for a candidate. They are voting for a group of **delegates,** or representatives, who will go to the party's **national convention,** or meeting, during the summer. Each delegate will cast one vote for the candidate he or she has agreed to support. The number of delegates each state will send to the convention depends on the population of the state—the bigger the state, the more delegates it will send. To make matters even more complicated, some states have a "winner take all" policy, which means that the candidate who gets the most votes in a particular state gets *all* its delegates' votes at the convention. In other states, the delegates' votes can be divided.

Not every state holds primary elections. The state of Iowa, for example, holds a **caucus,** which is a private meeting of the leaders of a political party. Leaders of each party in the state choose a presidential candidate to support for the nomination.

During the summer before a presidential election, the Democratic and Republican parties hold their national conventions, at which each party chooses one candidate for president.

A national convention takes place in a large indoor arena or convention hall, usually in a large city. The atmosphere is dramatic and spirited, and the convention goes on for several days. Thousands of people attend the national conventions. Some of them are delegates, sent to the convention by their states. In the main convention area, thousands of delegates and other excited party members gather, chat, and wear or carry signs that show their support for the individuals they wish to nominate. In addition, hundreds of news reporters are present. American flags hang everywhere. Overhead, red, white, and blue balloons are tied in clumps, waiting to be released when the party's candidate for president is announced.

Before the candidate is chosen, each party will develop what is called the party's **platform**—a statement of ideas and opinions the party will support in the upcoming election. The **planks** in the platform will be the individual issues that make up the platform. Some typical planks in a party's platform would be the party's ideas about health care, the environment, taxes, education, and gun control.

National Progressive Convention, Chicago, August 6, 1912

The high point of the convention begins when an announcer calls out the name of each state, beginning with Alabama and proceeding in alphabetical order. When each state's name is called, one of its delegates speaks into a microphone and announces the state's choice of presidential candidate—or how many delegates from the state are voting for each candidate. Party workers keep a running <u>tally</u> of the number of delegates who vote for each candidate. Eventually, one candidate has enough votes to claim victory. At this moment, a great cheer goes up as the colored balloons fly through the air, flags wave, and music plays.

In a short while, the party's official candidate for president comes to the microphone to accept the nomination and to give a speech. The chosen candidate also announces the name of a **running mate**—the person who will run for vice president. The candidates for president and vice president together are called the party's **ticket.**

The Presidential Campaign

At this point, the long journey to the presidential election has just begun. During the end of summer and the month of October, the Democratic and Republican candidates for president continue their campaigns. Now they face off against one another, instead of against other candidates from their own parties. Often another candidate, representing a third party, appears in <u>debates</u> and other preelection activities. The candidates travel around the country, talking to people and giving speeches, attempting to win votes. Finally, in early November, Americans vote in the general election.

Voting

Here is the usual way that U.S. citizens cast their votes. A citizen who is at least eighteen years old goes to a voting place, which is often located in a city or town building, a school, or a church. There the citizen finds <u>volunteers</u> ready to give instructions on how to mark the **ballot,** or list of candidates. There are several different methods of casting a vote. In some places, a voter writes on a paper ballot with a pencil or pen. In other places, a voter turns small levers next to the names of candidates on a voting machine. In still others, he or she punches out small holes next to the names of candidates on a paper ballot. (Plans are under way to replace these older voting methods with computerized voting.) While studying the ballot and making choices, the voter stands in a small cubicle surrounded with a curtain for privacy. In the United States, everyone's ballot is secret. No one has the right to know how anyone has voted unless the voter chooses to reveal his or her choices.

The Vote

Most people are surprised when they first learn that the **popular vote,** or the actual number of votes, does

Man entering voting booth (photo by Lewis Walker, Maryland, 1940s)

not always determine who wins a presidential election. To win the election, a presidential candidate must collect 270 **electoral votes** from a group of individuals known as the electoral college. The electoral vote, which occurs in January following the election, is the final step in the election of a president.

The **electoral college** is a group of representatives, or **electors,** from the fifty states plus the District of Columbia. (The electors are not the same people as the convention delegates.) Each state is given two electors plus the number of its representatives in the House. Since the number of representatives a state has is based on the state's population, the larger states have more electors and, therefore, more voting power. For example, in 2000, the state of California, which has fifty-two representatives in Congress, had fifty-four electoral votes, whereas the state of Maine, with two representatives in Congress, had only four electoral votes.

The presidential election of 2000 caused great controversy over the electoral college. Democrat Al Gore received more popular votes than Republican George W. Bush did. However, Bush won all the electoral votes from several large states, giving him 271 electoral votes, whereas Gore won 266. Thus, Bush won the election, despite the fact that fewer citizens actually voted for him than for Gore.

Electing Senators and Representatives

The campaign process for people who wish to win their parties' nominations for senator or representative is much like the campaign process for president. However, the interest in any one campaign is mostly limited to the state in which the particular election will take place and the campaign does not usually cost as much money. The main difference between electing a president and electing a senator or member of the House of Representatives is that both the primary and the general elections are **direct elections.** This means that, in both the primary and the general elections, voters vote directly for their favorite candidates rather than for delegates or electors. One more difference is the term of office. The president's **term of office,** or length of time in office, is four years, which may be followed by another four years if the president is reelected. After a second four-year term in office, a president may not run again. A senator's term of office is six years, and a representative's is two years. There is a general election for all the members of the House of

Representatives and for one-third of the Senate every two years—every even-numbered year. There is no limit on the number of times senators or representatives may be reelected.

OTHER WAYS TO INFLUENCE GOVERNMENT

Voting is not the only way to influence government. Individuals may write letters and e-mails to their representatives in Congress or express their views in letters to newspapers. Or they may write **petitions**—letters to government leaders that have been signed by many people. But people who have a strong interest in one particular issue have more power to influence government if they form an **interest group.** For example, paper manufacturers might benefit from laws allowing them to cut down trees in certain protected forest areas of the country. To try to influence government officials, the interest group hires **lobbyists**—professionals who are paid to meet with senators, representatives, governors, and other political leaders in an effort to persuade them to <u>initiate</u> and pass legislation that will support the needs of their employers. On the other hand, another special interest group that is concerned with protecting the environment might hire lobbyists to convince those same leaders that a law allowing trees to be cut down should not be passed.

While special interest groups use the media—newspapers, radio, and television—to help them influence government action, they rely most heavily on direct contact with the nation's political leaders. For this reason, most lobbyists live near Washington, D.C., so that they can have face-to-face contact as often as possible with the people who hold political power.

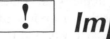 **! Implications**

To answer the question, "Why does all this matter?" or "What does it mean?," share the following insights with your child.

- *Politics is not a bad word.* Over time, the word politics has gathered a variety of negative associations, including dishonesty, the making of promises that will never be kept, and "smear campaigns," in which competing politicians say negative and often damaging things about each other. Although politics certainly has its negative aspects, it plays an important positive role in our democracy. Politics provides the arena for people with different ideas to compete for power in government—and to make their ideas and strengths known to the public. It is the complicated and often messy political process that gives the people in a democracy a way to freely choose their leaders and influence them once they are in office. After all, every citizen of age eighteen or older is a potential voter.

- **The power of the federal government has been a theme in American government since the earliest history of the United States.** It seems now, as it did in our nation's early history, that those who oppose "big government" want to protect the rights of individuals and of states from a federal government that might want to limit those rights. In contrast, others support a strong central government that has the power to step in and protect people's individual liberties from other individuals and from

individual states. For example, in the 1950s, many people wanted the federal government to step in and protect African Americans from discrimination by forcing schools to integrate; those opposed to "big government" did not think that the federal government should tell the states how to run their public schools.

- **The electoral college makes it possible for a candidate to become president without winning the popular vote.** Many feel that the electoral college should be eliminated—that a straight popular vote would be a better indication of the voice of the people. And yet others disagree. They say that the electoral college protects people who live in states with smaller populations by forcing politicians to pay attention to those states and the needs of their citizens. Even if a candidate carried every state that had twenty or more electors, that candidate would have only 189 electoral votes. The candidate would have to carry many smaller states to get the 270 electoral votes needed to win. Because of the electoral college, candidates cannot simply appeal to the big states with large urban populations and ignore the smaller states populated mainly by farmers.

 # Fact Checker

To check that your child knows or can find the basic facts in this chapter, here is a fill-in activity that requires a grasp of the political process as described in this chapter.

Complete this paragraph by filling in the blanks. Each of the answers is a word that appears in boldface type and is defined in this chapter. Look back in the chapter to find any words you're not sure of.

Years before a presidential election, people who want to become presidential (1.)_____ start getting ready for their (2.)_____. At first, they have to compete against other people in their own political (3.)_____. After each major party in each state chooses the person it wants to run, usually by holding a (4.)_____ election, each state will send (5.)_____ to a national (6.)_____. Each party will choose one candidate to run for president. Each of those candidates will choose a running (7.)_____ to run for vice president. When it is time for the (8.)_____ election, people will not really vote directly for the person they want to win. Instead, they will vote for a group of (9.)_____ from the electoral college. The person who wins the most (10.)_____ votes will become president, even if that person did not receive the most (11.)_____ votes.

Answers appear in the back, preceding the index.

The Big Questions

The following questions encourage your child to think critically rather than simply recall facts. If necessary, review the specific information from the preceding pages that will help your child make the necessary inferences to come up with reasonable answers.

1. If you were old enough to vote, do you have an idea about which party you would support—the Democrats or the Republicans? If you have already made your choice, what are your reasons?
2. Do you think we should do away with the electoral college? Give reasons for your opinion.
3. Is there an issue that is important to you but that is not addressed by either of the major parties? Suppose you were going to start a

third party? What issue would your party support? What would you name your party?

Suggested Answers

1. *Accept any answer as long as your child has sensible reasons for his or her choice. If your child is not ready to choose a party, you might direct him or her to newspaper articles or radio and TV news shows that would provide material on which to base such a choice. The descriptions in this chapter of the two major parties' basic views on government should help as well.*
2. *Either opinion is acceptable as long as your child has reasons for his or her opinion. Encourage your child to think about the problems that would be created by keeping or by doing away with the electoral college and how those problems could be solved.*
3. *Any issue is acceptable if it is one that is not addressed by either major party. Children should understand that the purpose of a third party is to provide voters with choices they would not have with only the two major parties to choose from.*

Skills Practice

The following activities give your child practice in applying the skills basic to social studies. For some of the activities, your child may need to review the information in the preceding pages.

A. USING SOCIAL STUDIES VOCABULARY

This activity gives your child a chance to use words that have specific meanings in the context of social studies in a more general way.

The five words in the word bank have special meanings when used to talk about politics and elections. They are also used in a more general way in ordinary conversation, as in the sentences that follow. In each of these sentences, fill in the blank with a word from the word bank.

Word Bank

candidate	politician	popular
	campaigning	delegates

1. My parents call my brother the _____ of the family because he knows how to get everyone to agree with him.
2. The students in my class are _____ to get our teacher to stop giving homework over the weekend.
3. I can't decide whether to have chocolate or strawberry ice cream—they are both good _____.
4. Our class sent two students as _____ to the principal's office to ask for permission to go on a trip.
5. Our dog is a golden retriever, which is one of the _____ kinds of dog.

Answers

(1.) politician; (2.) campaigning; (3.) candidates; (4.) delegates; (5.) popular

Evaluating Your Child's Skills: In order to complete this activity successfully, your child's understanding of the vocabulary words on the list must be thorough enough so that he or she can use the specific political meaning of each word to figure out a more general way to use the word. If necessary, help your child make comparisons between political situations in which the words would be used and ordinary situations in the sentences. For example, a person who is *campaigning* is trying to persuade others to do what he or she wants, whether it is voting or cutting back on homework.

B.   WRITING AN EXPLANATION

This activity gives your child practice in explaining in writing a complex idea so that another person can understand it. Students are often asked to do this in order to answer essay questions on written tests.

In one paragraph, explain in writing how the electoral college works. You do not have to give your opinion about the electoral college or tell how it can affect presidential elections. Simply explain how it works.

Suggested Answers

When people vote in a presidential election, they don't really vote for the candidates. They vote for a group of electors in the electoral college. The number of electors each state has equals the number of that state's senators, which is always two, plus the number of the state's representatives in the House, which is based on the state's population. The candidate with the most electoral votes wins.

Evaluating Your Child's Skills: In order to complete this activity successfully, your child must have not only a complete understanding of the electoral college, but the ability to explain clearly in writing the complex way the electoral college works. If your child's answer shows a lack of understanding, review with him or her the necessary facts. If any part of your child's answer is confusing or unclear, help him or her revise in order to clarify.

MAKING A TIMELINE

The following activity asks your child to use a graphic organizer to put events in order.

The following list names four events that occur during a presidential election year in the United States. Place each event in the proper place on the following timeline.

general election
national conventions
electoral college vote
primary elections

winter to spring   summer   November   December

36

Answers

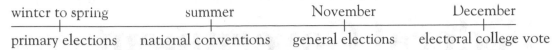

winter to spring   summer   November   December

primary elections   national conventions   general elections   electoral college vote

Evaluating Your Child's Skills: **In order to complete this activity successfully, your child needs to have a good mental picture of the stages of a presidential election and how a presidential election progresses. He or she also needs to see the relationships among the events. If necessary, show your child the portions of the text that explain the events on the timeline in relation to one another.**

 # Top of the Class

Children interested in delving more deeply into the topic of this chapter can choose one or more of the following activities. They may do the activities for their own satisfaction or share what they have done in class to show that they have been seriously considering the topic of the political process in the United States.

A POINT TO PONDER

Encourage your child to consider why many people don't vote and whether voting should be compulsory.

Free elections are essential to a democratic way of life, and most Americans consider the right to vote one of our most precious liberties. Yet many Americans don't take the time or trouble to vote—even in presidential elections. Do you have any ideas about why this is true? What if voting were required by law? Do you think that would be a good idea? What are your ideas on the subject of voting?

It might be interesting to raise these questions in class and see what your classmates think.

ELECTION WATCHING

If a national election is taking place, encourage your child to find out as much as possible about it.

Is this a year for a presidential election? If not, is there an election going on this year for the Senate or House of Representatives in your state or congressional district? If so, follow the campaigns and the issues closely. Keep a clipping file of newspaper articles. Take notes on debates or campaign ads you see on television. Decide which candidate you would vote for and why. You might even do some campaigning yourself with friends or relatives who are old enough to vote.

BOOKS TO READ

Suggest that your child read one of the following nonfiction books and respond to it by offering an oral or written critique in class.

Fradin, Dennis B. *Voting and Elections.* Children's Press, 1985. A simplified explanation for younger children.

Gutman, Dan. *Landslide! A Kid's Guide to the U.S. Elections.* Aladdin Paperbacks (Simon & Schuster Children's Publishing Division), 2000. Upbeat. Question-and-answer format.

Harvey, Miles. *Presidential Elections* (*Cornerstones of Freedom* series). Children's Press, 1995. A solid reference for children in grades 4 to 6.

CHAPTER 4

Federal Government: The Legislative Branch

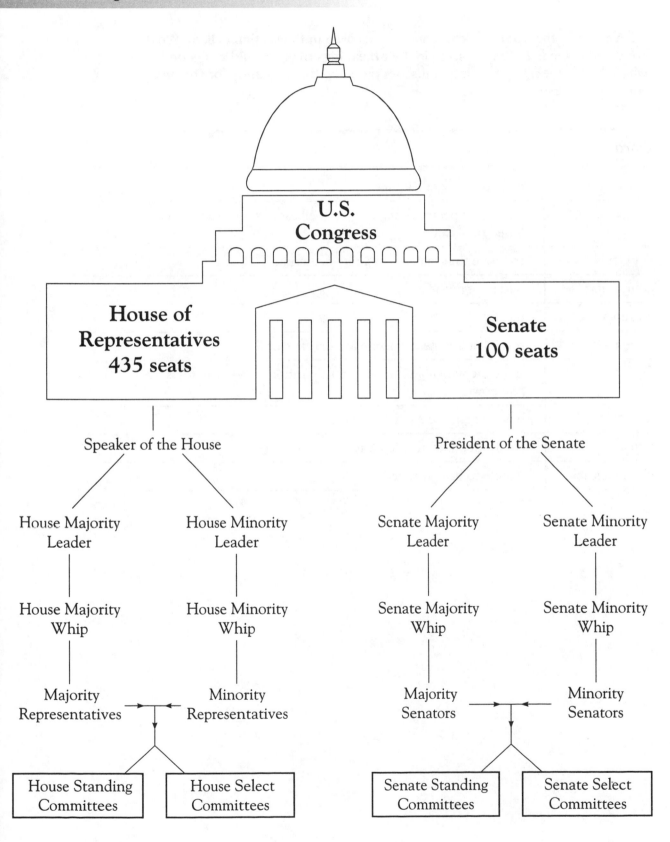

Word Power

The words on the following chart are underscored in the section called "What Your Child Needs to Know." Explain their meanings to your child as needed when they come up in reading or discussion. Keep the list handy for you and your child to use.

Word	*Definition*
accusation	a charge of wrongdoing
aristocracy	a group of people thought to be the best in some way, usually based on wealth
convict	to prove that someone is guilty of a crime
counterfeit	false; not authentic
currency	money
designates	names or chooses someone for an office or duty
figurehead	someone who holds an important position or office but has no real power
populous	having many people living there
sparsely	thinly, in an uncrowded way
unmanageable	unable to be controlled

What Your Child Needs to Know

You may choose to use the following text in several different ways, depending on your child's strengths and preferences. You might read the passage aloud; you might read it to yourself and then paraphrase it for your child; or you might ask your child to read the material along with you or on his or her own.

INTRODUCTION TO THE LEGISLATIVE BRANCH

The legislative branch of our government is the branch that makes laws. The name for that branch is the U.S. Congress. Congress is made up of two parts, or houses: the Senate and the House of Representatives. Members of the Senate are elected for six-year terms, while representatives are elected for two-year terms, but there is no limit on the number of times a senator or a representative may be reelected.

This chapter explains the way American citizens are represented in Congress. It also explains the complex process by which our government makes laws.

THE BRITISH MODEL

As noted in Chapter 1, the idea for the structure of the U.S. government did not spring suddenly from the ground of the thirteen colonies. It was planned carefully and based on an already existing model—the British Parliament.

The colonists knew they wished to build a government similar to the one in England. Parliament was (and remains) bicameral, or divided into two separate governing bodies. The House of Lords was also known as the "upper house" because its representatives were members of the aristocracy. The House of Commons, known as the "lower house," was made up of businessmen, landowners, and other "commoners." Most important, England had a representative government; that is, members of Parliament—those who were actually engaged in

Capitol Building, Washington, D.C.

Houses of Parliament, London

the business of making laws—represented the wishes and interests of large groups of people.

HOW ARE AMERICAN CITIZENS REPRESENTED IN CONGRESS?

American citizens are represented in both houses of Congress, but in different ways. The Senate and the House of Representatives are organized so as to balance each other in a way that is fair to all of the nation's citizens.

In the Senate, each of the fifty states is represented by two senators, regardless of the state's population. Thus, in the Senate, the voting power of small or <u>sparsely</u> populated states, such as Delaware and Wyoming, equals the voting power of large or <u>populous</u> states like Florida and New York. The Senate's structure embodies the idea that all states are equally important. For example, both Texas, with a population of about 17 million, and Alaska, with a population of about half a million, have two votes in the Senate. Each of Texas's two senators could be said to represent about 8.5 million citizens—half of the state's total population. Using the same yardstick, one could say that each of Alaska's senators represents 250,000 peo-

ple. In the Senate, then, each state has the same amount of power, but a single Alaskan citizen has more political "muscle" than a Texan citizen does, since each senator represents a smaller number of people.

On the other hand, in the House of Representatives, each state's voting power is determined by its population. States with more people have more votes than states with fewer people. This structure embodies the idea that the voting power of all individual citizens should be equal, even if the states are unequal in power. For example, in 2001, the nation's most populous state, California, had fifty-two representatives. Nevada, the least populous state, had only one. But each representative in both states represented approximately the same number of voters.

Apportioning Seats in the House

In the decades leading up to 1929, the total membership of the House grew as rapidly as the nation's population. Finally the number of representatives reached 435. Political leaders realized that the House could become <u>unmanageable</u> and unable to govern if it grew too large. Consequently, Congress passed a law limiting the House to 435 members (or **seats**). Despite the fact that the country's population has continued to grow since 1929, the number of seats in the House is frozen at 435.

However, a state does not necessarily always have the same number of representatives. If the population of a state grows, it will gain a representative, whereas if the population gets smaller, it will lose a representative. But the total number of representatives in the house remains the same. This is carried out by congressional districting.

Congressional Districting

Most representatives do not represent their entire state, but the citizens who live in one particular part of the state. Each state is divided into **congressional districts**—one district, or area, for each representative. If a state gains or loses representatives, of course, it must redraw the boundaries of its congressional districts. Instead of being divided into three regions, for instance, a state whose population is growing might need to divide itself into four regions. Today all congressional districts are divided into approximately 575,000 people.

Senate Leaders

Both houses of Congress must have leaders in order to function effectively. The Constitution states that the nation's vice president, although not a senator, will lead the Senate and be known as its president. In reality, the vice president has little power in this particular role, acting primarily as a <u>figurehead</u> who keeps Senate sessions running smoothly. Ordinarily, the vice president does not vote on issues in the Senate but, in case of a tie, casts the tie-breaking vote.

Each major party has its own leader in the Senate. These two individuals are called the **Senate majority leader** and the **Senate minority leader,** according to which party holds the majority of seats in the Senate. (If the number of Democrats and Republicans in the Senate is equal, the leaders are simply called **Senate Republican leader** and **Senate Democratic leader.**) The leader of each party is elected by senators from his or her own party. In addition, each party <u>designates</u> members called **whips**—the majority whip and the minority whip—to make sure that party members are present on the Senate floor during important voting sessions.

House Leadership

The House is set up similarly to the Senate. The leader of the House of Representatives is called the **Speaker of the House.** The Speaker is elected by the members of the majority party. The Speaker holds a great deal of power in the House. While running daily House sessions, the Speaker determines who can address the members of the House. In addition, the Speaker decides which representatives will serve on committees and when issues will be discussed and voted on. Furthermore, if both the president and vice president were unable to serve due to illness or death, the Speaker of the House would automatically become president.

As in the Senate, each party in the House has its leaders. The majority and minority leaders, as well as whips, are chosen by each party's representatives.

Congressional Committees

Each of the two houses of Congress votes as one body. However, most of Congress's daily work is done not as a group of 100 senators or 435 representatives, but rather in committees of a dozen or so members.

Standing committees are permanent organizations that focus on particular topics, such as agriculture, the budget, and energy and natural resources. Standing committees continue as individual members come and go; they are fixtures in both the House and the Senate. Though committees are sometimes added or dropped, the Senate usually has about fifteen, and the House usually has about twenty. Some of the topics handled by standing committees are large and complicated. For this reason, many **subcommittees,** or smaller committees, are formed to study specialized topics in greater depth and detail.

Sometimes a special situation or issue arises that needs careful and immediate attention. In this case, the House or Senate may form a **select committee** to study the issue. Unlike a standing committee, a select committee exists only as long as it takes to address or solve the subject at hand. Typically, this process takes anywhere from a few months to a few years.

THE POWERS OF CONGRESS

The framers of the Constitution knew that they had to give Congress broad powers in order to limit the powers of the presidency—to be sure that no president would ever become an absolute ruler. On the other hand, they also knew that they had to limit the powers of Congress to prevent the legislature from passing unfair laws that would take away the people's liberties. In the Constitution, therefore, they **enumerated,** or specifically named, the powers that would be given to Congress. Some of these powers are legislative—they pertain to the actual process of making laws; others are nonlegislative; still others are called *additional* or *implied* powers. All of the powers discussed in the following paragraphs are enumerated in Article I, Section 8, of the Constitution.

Legislative Powers

Most of the powers granted to the Senate and the House of Representatives concern legislation.

- *Congress makes laws relating to taxation.* The government needs money to run itself. Most of this money is collected from U.S. citizens in the form of taxes. (See Chapter 8.)
- *Congress makes laws allowing the government to borrow the money it needs in order to run smoothly.* The government sells savings bonds and Treasury notes as a way of borrowing extra money from citizens. When an individual buys a government savings bond, he or she is actually lending money to the government. After a certain number of years, the person cashes in the bond, receiving the amount paid for it plus the **interest,** or extra money, it has earned. In the meanwhile, the government has been able to use that money to run its programs. (See Chapter 8.)
- *Congress makes laws relating to the production and regulation of money.* Since 1789, the United States has had a stable system of <u>currency</u> in which only money issued by the federal government can be used. Congress has passed laws making the manufacture of <u>counterfeit</u> money a crime and calling for the punishment of counterfeiters.
- *Congress makes laws regulating interstate commerce, or trade between states.* The Constitution states that "Congress shall have Power . . . To regulate Commerce . . . among the several States. . . ." Almost every business engages, in some way, in interstate commerce—even a business that buys or sells food that has crossed

state lines, for example. Congress has used this power to make important laws ensuring that any business must pay its workers a minimum wage and that no business can practice any kind of discrimination against its employees or against the public.

- *Congress makes laws affecting naturalization and citizenship.* The federal legislature, not the individual states, controls immigration to the United States by people from other countries. (See Chapter 2.)
- *Congress makes laws that establish and maintain post offices.* The federal government, rather than the states, has the power and the responsibility to protect the mail and to see that it is collected and delivered correctly all around the nation.
- *As part of the government's system of checks and balances (see Chapter 1), Congress has powers relating to other governmental branches.* For instance, it is Congress that makes laws determining how many justices should serve on the U.S. Supreme Court. In addition, Congress creates legislation that defines federal crimes and their punishments.
- *Congress has many powers relating to national defense and foreign relations.* It is only Congress—not the president—that oversees trade with other nations and creates and maintains armed forces. Of course, some issues involving foreign relations require the executive and legislative branches to share power. According to the Constitution, for example, only Congress can declare war on another country. But the decision to send American armed forces into combat without a formal declaration of war is sometimes made by presidents. For example, in the cases of the Korean, Vietnam, and Gulf wars, Presidents Truman, Kennedy, and George H. Bush sent troops to foreign soil before asking the houses of Congress for permission to use American troops in a foreign conflict. Eventually, Congress passed the **War Powers Act,** which states that a president may not continue sending troops to foreign soil for more than sixty days without permission from Congress.

Nonlegislative Powers

Some of Congress's powers do not relate to creating or passing laws. The following are examples of Congress's most important nonlegislative powers.

- *Congress can impeach and remove any member of the executive or judicial branch of the U.S. government.* **Impeachment** is a formal <u>accusation</u> of wrongdoing in office. A government official can be impeached only by a majority vote in the House. After impeachment, the Senate holds a trial. If two-thirds of the Senate votes to <u>convict</u> the accused official, he or she can be removed from office. Most impeachment cases have involved judges; however, two presidents (Andrew Johnson and Bill Clinton) have been impeached, though not convicted, by Congress.
- *The House of Representatives has the power to break ties in the electoral vote.* If no presidential candidate wins enough electoral votes for election, the House chooses the president. This situation has occurred only twice, when the House elected Thomas Jefferson in 1800 and John Quincy Adams in 1824.
- *Congress can propose amendments to the U.S. Constitution.* In fact, Congress has proposed all of the existing twenty-seven constitutional amendments, as well as six others that were not ratified.
- *Presidential appointments must be confirmed— and presidential treaties ratified—by the Senate.* Presidents have the power to appoint federal judges, but each of these appointments must be approved by a majority of the Senate. Similarly, two-thirds of the Senate must ratify **treaties,** or formal agreements, that presidents make with other nations.

Implied Powers

Congress claims additional powers from the **elastic clause** of the Constitution. This part of the Constitution states that Congress can take powers needed to run the government, even if these powers are not spelled out in the Constitution. Among the most important of these **implied powers** are Congress's **investigative powers.** That is, Congress has the power to conduct investigations into wrongdoing involving the U.S. government. In these cases, witnesses testify under oath before a congressional committee. One famous example of a congressional investigation is the Senate's Watergate Committee hearings of the 1970s. A Senate investigation established that people close to President Richard Nixon had been involved in a break-in at the Democratic Party's national headquarters in Washington, D.C. The facts uncovered by the investigation led to Nixon's resignation.

Another implied power of Congress is an example of checks and balances called **legislative oversight**—the power to see that the executive branch correctly carries out the laws that Congress has created.

Powers Denied to Congress

The Constitution specifically designates certain powers that are strictly denied to Congress.

- *Congress may not suspend a writ of habeas corpus.* A **writ** (RIT) **of habeas corpus** (HAY bee uhss KOR puhss) is a written order that a lawyer or friend of an arrested person can obtain from a judge. The writ says that the arresting police officer must appear in court along with the arrested person so that the court can decide whether the person was arrested for a legal reason. If the court decides that the person was illegally arrested, the person must be freed immediately. If a judge has granted a writ of habeas corpus, Congress does not have the right to disobey it.
- *Congress does not have the right to convict or punish a person accused of a crime unless the person is given a fair trial.* By denying this power to Congress, the right of every citizen to a fair trial is protected.
- *Congress may not pass ex post facto (EKS pohst FAK toh) laws.* An **ex post facto** (after the fact) **law** is one that makes a crime out of an act that was legal before the law was passed. A person cannot be punished for doing something that was legal at the time he or she did that thing, even though, later on, a law may be passed against the action.

LAWMAKING: BILLS AND RESOLUTIONS

Every year, tens of thousands of **bills,** or proposed laws, are introduced in Congress. Yet only a few hundred of these bills become laws. The basic reason for this is the complicated and time-consuming process needed to make laws. Lawmakers must be willing to change minor details of a bill—sometimes over and over again—before they can satisfy the members of Congress who must support the bill in order for it to become a law. If the supporters of a bill are unable to compromise with other lawmakers who disagree with the bill or with parts of it, the bill is almost sure to die before becoming law.

A Bill Is Born

Here are the early steps that a bill must take on the long road to becoming law.

- The process begins with an idea for solving some problem. An idea for a new law might come from a senator or representative, from a citizen who has written a letter to a senator or representative, from an interest group, or from the president.
- The senator or representative prepares a bill— a written explanation of the idea. If the bill is prepared by a senator, it will be introduced in the Senate; if by a representative, it will be introduced in the House.
- If the bill is being prepared for the House, the representative drops it into a hopper—a box used to collect bills. In the Senate, a senator makes a formal announcement of the new bill.

The Bill Is Handed to a Committee

- The bill is assigned to the standing committee that most closely fits its subject. For example, a senator's bill to give elementary schools money to buy computers might be given to a subcommittee of the Senate Health, Education, Labor, and Pensions Committee. The subcommittee studies the bill and takes one of four actions: it recommends that the bill be passed exactly as it appears; it changes the bill and sends it back to the Senate or the House; it "kills" the bill immediately; it lets the bill "die" by setting it aside for an indefinite amount of time. This last action describes the way most congressional bills end up.
- If a committee wishes to recommend that a bill be passed into law, first the committee must hold public hearings. Government officials, experts on the bill's subject, and lobbyists and other representatives of special interest groups usually try to have the bill changed in different ways.
- After the committee has agreed to any changes, the members vote to kill the bill or to **report** it **out,** which means to send it to the full House or Senate—depending on where it originated—for consideration.

The Bill Goes Back to the House or the Senate

- A reported bill must be scheduled on a congressional calendar. In the Senate, bills are usually handled fairly quickly. However, the much larger House has five separate calendars to schedule different types of bills. The House Rules Committee oversees such scheduling, and this committee can purposely speed up or slow down bills by scheduling them ahead of others or behind them.
- Finally, a bill is discussed by the entire House or Senate. Now legislators have a chance to debate specific aspects of the bill. Unlike their colleagues in the House, senators can speak as long as they like on the Senate floor during the debate period. In fact, one way to kill a bill in the Senate is to talk continually for many hours or even days about the bill and related topics. This strategy is called a **filibuster.** The only way to stop a filibuster is for three-fifths of the Senate to vote to limit speaking time for one hour. Filibustering—even the threat of a filibuster—often succeeds in killing a bill.
- After debate, representatives or senators vote to kill or pass a bill. In order for a vote to be taken, a majority of congressional members (in other words, 51 senators or 218 representatives) must be present. A bill must receive a majority of the votes of members present in order to pass.

The House and Senate Working Together

Before a bill becomes law, it must be passed by both the House and the Senate. If the bill originated in

House chamber, House of Representatives

President Bill Clinton signing a bill (National Voter Registration Act of 1993)

the House and the majority of the House voted in favor of it, it will then go to the Senate for a vote—or the other way around.

The Final Hurdle: The President

After a bill passes both houses of Congress, it is sent to the president. If the president signs the bill—or leaves it unsigned for ten days while Congress is in session—the bill becomes a law. If the president leaves it unsigned for ten days while Congress is *not* in session, the bill is considered dead. If the president vetoes, or formally rejects it, the bill is dead. However, Congress can **override,** or reverse, a veto if two-thirds of both the House and Senate vote to do so. Though overrides are rare, they do sometimes turn bills into laws.

 Implications

To answer the question, "Why does all this matter?" or "What does it mean?," share the following insights with your child.

- **The denial of certain powers to Congress prevents the United States from becoming a "police state."** The framers of the Constitution knew that Congress needed broad powers in order to operate effectively—thus the elastic clause, granting Congress what we call implied

powers. But they also showed great wisdom by strictly denying certain powers—seeing to it that these powers could not come under the elastic clause. The framers had the wisdom to know that even U.S. citizens may need to be protected from their own government.

- **Laws in the United States are created by 535 people rather than by only a few.** Although an idea is generated by an individual, ultimately that idea must be generally acceptable to many people who represent the American public before it can pass into law. This is about as far as you can get from an absolute dictatorship in which one single person or just a few powerful people have the right to make laws that everyone must obey.

- **Nearly every bill that is passed into law represents compromise.** Before a bill can even make it to the House or the Senate, it is usually changed many times before it is considered satisfactory to be placed in the hopper at the House of Representatives or reported out to the Senate. Refusal to compromise means almost certain death for a bill. This spirit of compromise is at the heart of our democracy. Citizens of a democracy understand that it is impossible for every person to agree on every detail of every law, but that taking the time and trouble to make every law as acceptable as possible to the greatest number of people is well worth the time and effort.

Fact Checker

To check that your child knows or can find the basic facts in this chapter, here is a categorizing activity that requires a grasp of Congress's different types of powers as described in this chapter.

Place each of the following items in the correct column in the chart.

make tax laws

impeach a government leader

suspend writ of habeas corpus

regulate interstate commerce

make immigration laws

break ties in the electoral college

investigative powers

make ex post facto laws

propose constitutional amendments

legislative oversight

convict a person without a trial

Legislative Powers	Nonlegislative Powers	Implied Powers	Denied Powers

Answers appear in the back, preceding the index.

The Big Questions

The following questions encourage your child to think critically rather than simply recall facts. If necessary, review the specific information from the preceding pages that will help your child make the necessary inferences to come up with reasonable answers.

1. In times of extreme national emergency, should any of the powers denied to Congress be allowed, just temporarily, to ensure the safety of U.S. citizens? For example, after thousands of innocent people were killed in the 2001 terrorist attack on the World Trade Cen-ter in New York City, should Congress have temporarily been given the power to suspend writs of habeas corpus with regard to suspected terrorists?

2. Our legislature is modeled on the British Parliament, which also has two houses—the House of Lords, or upper house, and the House of Commons, or lower house. While we have no aristocracy in the United States, can you think of any reason for identifying the U.S. Senate as the upper house of our legislature and the House of Representatives as the lower house?

Suggested Answers

1. *Accept any opinion, as long as it is well reasoned. But you might want to suggest that once such an*

important rule has been suspended, it may be broken again—perhaps in a situation in which the suspending of the rule seems less justified.
2. In the Senate, each state has equal representation, but people are not equally represented. In the

House of Representatives, each citizen has equal representation because the more populous states have more representatives. Therefore, the House of Representatives can be thought of as "the people's house."

Skills Practice

The following activities give your child practice in applying the skills basic to social studies. For some of the activities, your child may need to review the information in the preceding pages.

A. COMPARING AND CONTRASTING

Make sure your child understands that *comparing* means finding similarities, or likenesses, between two things or ideas and *contrasting* means finding differences. Then have your child note at least one important similarity or difference in the following pairs. (Note: You might also explain to your child that the word *compare* in everyday conversation often means "show both similarities and differences.")

To compare, explain at least one important similarity between the members of each of the following pairs. To contrast, explain at least one important difference.

1. The British Parliament and the U.S. Congress (compare)
2. The U.S. Senate and the House of Representatives (contrast)
3. The president of the Senate (the vice president) and the Speaker of the House (contrast)
4. A bill introduced in the Senate and a bill introduced in the House (compare)

Suggested Answers

1. *Both are bicameral; in both, the members represent the people.*
2. *In the Senate, there are two senators from each state; in the House of Representatives, the number of representatives from a state is based on the state's population.*

3. *The president of the Senate (the vice president) has little power in the Senate, with the exception of the power to cast a tie-breaking vote; the Speaker of the House is actually a representative and has a powerful role in the House of Representatives, including determining who can address the house and who will serve on committees.*
4. *Whether a bill is introduced in the Senate or in the House of Representatives, it must be approved by a majority in the house in which it was introduced, then be approved by a majority in the other house, and then by the president.*

Evaluating Your Child's Skills: In order to complete this activity successfully, your child needs to put together pieces of information that may be stated in different parts of the text. For example, the powers of the president of the Senate and the Speaker of the House are discussed in separate paragraphs. If your child has trouble, suggest that he or she go back to the "What Your Child Needs to Know" section, locate the needed information, and then look for similarities and differences.

B. SUPPORTING GENERAL STATEMENTS WITH SPECIFIC FACTS

Ask your child to read the following statements about what he or she has learned. Identify the statements as *general statements*—statements that may be true but that need specific facts or examples to back them up. Have your child come up with at least one specific fact to back up each general statement. This skill is useful for both speaking and writing activities in all subjects.

1. Some people hold positions of leadership in both houses of Congress.
2. A bill goes through many stages before it becomes a law.
3. Some powers are denied to Congress by the Constitution.

Suggested Answers

1. *The vice president is president of the Senate; the Speaker of the House is the leader of the House of Representatives. In addition, in each house of Congress, both major parties have their own leaders and whips.*
2. *After a bill is introduced, it goes to a committee, goes through public hearings, goes back to the committee for revision, goes to the house in which it was introduced for a vote, goes to the other house for a vote, and goes to the president for approval. If vetoed by the president, the bill can still go back to Congress, which can override the president's veto by a two-thirds majority vote in each house.*
3. *Congress may not suspend a writ of habeas corpus, convince or punish an accused person without a trial, or pass an ex post facto law.*

Evaluating Your Child's Skills: In order to complete this activity successfully, your child needs to be able to distinguish between general statements and specific facts. Your child also must develop the ability to use specific facts to support general statements. If necessary, model the skill by making a general statement about your family's everyday life and asking your child to support the statement with specific factual examples.

Top of the Class

Children interested in delving more deeply into the topic of this chapter can choose one or more of the following activities. They may do the activities for their own satisfaction or share what they have done in class to show that they have been seriously considering the workings of the legislative branch of the federal government.

CONGRESS TODAY

Encourage your child to find out how people in your area are represented in Congress.

Use resources in your library or on the Internet to find out how you and your neighbors are represented in Congress. Make a list like the one that follows, and then complete it with the appropriate names.

In addition, if you would like to communicate with your representative in Congress, find the address, telephone number, and e-mail address of his or her office. If you have any opinions to express or suggestions to make, you are welcome to do so.

President of the Senate
Senate Majority Leader
Senate Minority Leader
Senate Majority Whip
Senate Minority Whip
Speaker of the House
House Majority Leader
House Minority Leader
House Majority Whip
House Minority Whip
Names of senators from your state (2)
Number of representatives in your state
Name of your representative in Congress

A POINT TO PONDER

Encourage your child to think about why there are no limits on the number of times senators and representatives can be reelected—and about whether there should be.

In 1978, a constitutional amendment was proposed to limit the number of years a member of Congress can serve to twelve. The amendment was not accepted, but the issue is still debated.

The main reason for supporting term limits is that most senators and representatives are re-elected, which makes it difficult for new people with new ideas to serve in Congress. The main reason for not supporting term limits is that term limits would deny voters the opportunity to vote for someone they already know and trust. Think about whether or not you support term limits. You may want to discuss the issue in class.

BOOKS TO READ

Suggest that your child read one of the following nonfiction books and respond to it by offering an oral or written critique in class.

Gourse, Leslie. *The Congress* (*First Books* series). Watts, 1995. The powers of the legislative branch and a history of both houses.

Sendak, Cass R. *Congressional Committees* (*Inside Government* series). Twenty-First Century, 1995. An illustrated explanation of how congressional committees work.

Weber, Michael. *Our Congress* (*I Know America* series). Millbrook, 1994. A history of Congress, its structure, and its functions.

CHAPTER 5

Federal Government: The Judicial Branch

Supreme Court Bldg. - Washington, D.C.

The judicial branch of the federal government includes the U.S. Supreme Court, the thirteen U.S. courts of appeals, and ninety-one district courts. In addition, it includes several other courts, such as the U.S. Tax Court and the U.S. Claims Court. This chart shows how the judicial branch of the government is organized.

THE FEDERAL COURT SYSTEM

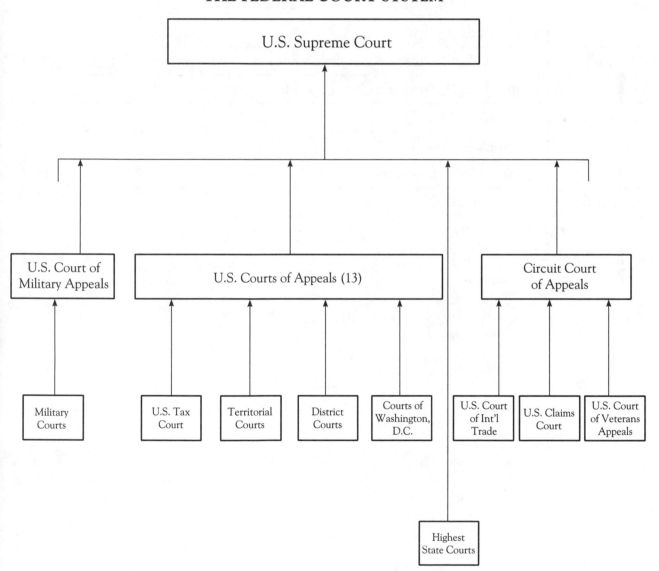

Word Power

Word	Definition
clients	people who hire lawyers to advise them or represent them in court
compensate	make up for
evidence	facts indicating that a person is guilty or innocent of a crime
fraud	the illegal cheating or tricking of people
ideological	relating to ideas
overturn	reverse, undo
recesses	takes a break from work
unanimous	agreed to by all

What Your Child Needs to Know

You may choose to use the following text in several different ways, depending on your child's strengths and preferences. You might read the passage aloud; you might read it to yourself and then paraphrase it for your child; or you might ask your child to read the material along with you or on his or her own.

INTRODUCTION TO THE JUDICIAL BRANCH

The judicial branch of the U.S. government is the branch that has the power to make **legal** decisions, or decisions regarding laws. Such decisions range from whether a person is guilty or not guilty of breaking a law to whether a law itself is unconstitutional. The judicial branch consists of a system of courts where judges hear many different kinds of cases argued by **attorneys,** or lawyers. All federal court judges are appointed by the president with the approval of the Senate and hold their appointments for life.

PRINCIPLES OF THE AMERICAN LEGAL SYSTEM

Our **legal system,** or system of courts, is built on four basic principles:

1. All people receive **equal justice under the law.** In other words, our legal system is intended to treat every person the same way, regardless of his or her age, race, sex, ethnic background, or economic status (wealth).
2. All people are guaranteed **due process of law.** This means that no one can be convicted of a crime without a fair and complete trial.
3. The best way to ensure fair trials is through an **adversary system** of justice. That is, lawyers, representing their <u>clients</u>, argue against each other, each presenting his or her side of the argument in the best way possible in order to win a case.

4. A **presumption of innocence** should underlie the treatment of suspects by the police as well as in the courts. In short, a person accused of a crime should be considered innocent until proven guilty.

BACKGROUND OF THE LEGAL SYSTEM IN THE UNITED STATES

The judicial branch of our government, like the legislative and executive branches, was provided for by the framers of the Constitution. But the Constitution says little about how the judicial branch should function or be organized. In fact, Article III of the Constitution specifically establishes only one court—the U.S. Supreme Court. It grants Congress the power to create additional federal courts.

THE FUNCTION OF THE FEDERAL COURTS

In this chapter, we discuss the structure and operation of the **federal courts,** the courts operated by the federal government, ranging from lower courts all the way up to the **U.S. Supreme Court**—the nation's highest court. In Chapter 9, you will find information about the **state courts,** operated by the individual states according to their own state laws and state constitutions.

The **jurisdiction,** or authority, of the federal courts is different from that of the state courts. This means that the federal courts have the authority to hear certain kinds of cases, and the state courts have the authority to hear others. For instance, some crimes are **federal crimes**—crimes that are against laws made by the federal government. Kidnapping, violating a person's civil rights, mail <u>fraud</u>, and driving a stolen car from one state to another are all examples of federal crimes. Federal courts have jurisdiction over cases involving federal crimes only. Other crimes are **state crimes**—crimes that are against laws made by a particular state. A case involving state laws is *not* tried in a federal court, no matter how serious the crime. For example, there is no federal law against murder or robbery, although every state has laws against these crimes. Therefore, murder and robbery cases are not within the jurisdiction of the federal courts; rather, cases involving such crimes come under the authority of states and are tried in state courts.

In addition to the types of federal cases already mentioned, federal courts have jurisdiction in cases involving the following people or organizations:

- Any part of the U.S. government
- Two or more state governments
- Representatives of the governments of other nations
- Two or more individuals or businesses from different states

TYPES OF LAW HANDLED BY THE FEDERAL COURTS

The federal court system handles three different types of law.

- **Civil law** does not involve crime. Rather, it involves disagreements between two individuals or between an individual and the government. For example, a person who owns land near a river may claim that a factory up the river is dumping harmful chemicals into the water. If the two individuals—the person who owns the land and the person who owns the factory—cannot resolve the problem between themselves, one may choose to take the other to court. The landowner would probably ask the court to order the factory owner to stop polluting the river. In a different kind of case, one person might ask the court to order another to pay money to <u>compensate</u> for some sort of suffering or financial loss. The person making the complaint is called the **plaintiff;** the person against whom the complaint is made is called the **defendant.**
- **Criminal law** involves cases in which the federal government itself brings charges against a person for breaking a law. A person on trial for breaking a law is called the defendant.
- **Constitutional law** involves complaints by citizens or groups of citizens that existing laws limit rights guaranteed to them by the Constitution. In other words, cases of constitutional law concern whether or not a law violates the Constitution.

Attorney addressing a jury. (The man speaking is Fred W. Garmone, associate defense counsel, making the opening statement to the jury at Dr. Samuel Sheppard's trial for the murder of his wife, 1954. Sheppard and associate defense counsel Arthur Peterslige listen in the foreground. Artist: E. Kudlaty)

TYPES OF FEDERAL COURTS

The lower federal courts take two main forms: **district courts,** where all cases are first heard, and **appellate courts,** which hear **appeals,** or requests that decisions already made by district courts be reversed, or changed. In addition, other courts, called **legislative courts,** have been created by Congress to help the legislative branch of the government carry out its powers. Each type of court is briefly described in the following paragraphs.

District Courts

At present, there are ninety-one federal district courts in the United States. Each state has at least one federal district court, with more than one in the more populous states. District courts are the only courts that use **juries,** or groups of citizens, to make decisions on legal cases. Most adult U.S. citizens are required, every few years, to serve on a jury. There are two types of juries: a grand jury, which means large jury, and a petit jury, which means small jury.

A **grand jury** is a panel of sixteen to twenty-three citizens. Lawyers go before a grand jury to show that there is enough <u>evidence</u> against the accused person to bring the case to trial. The accused person's lawyer tries to show that there is not enough evidence. If the grand jury decides that enough evidence exists, the accused person will go to trial. Otherwise, the accused person is free.

If the accused person does go to trial, a **petit** (PET ee) **jury,** usually consisting of six to twelve citizens, is chosen. The lawyer for the defendant—the **defense attorney**—and the lawyer trying to prove the defendant is guilty—the **prosecuting attorney**—present evidence to the jury by questioning **witnesses**—people who have information regarding the case. Then the jury goes into a private room to discuss the case. Finally, the jury gives a **verdict,** or decision, that states whether they find the accused person not guilty or guilty. In most states, the verdict must be <u>unanimous</u>. Note that the judge does not decide on the verdict. The judge's responsibilities include making sure that the trial is conducted fairly, according to a set of very strict rules. The judge also decides on a convicted person's **sentence,** or punishment.

In civil cases, there is no grand jury. And in some civil cases, the people involved might prefer not to have the case decided by a jury. Then a panel of three federal district judges decides how the case will be settled.

Appellate Courts

If a person who has lost a case in a federal court wants to appeal the case, or try to have the decision reversed, he or she may bring the case to a higher court called an appellate court. Ordinary appeals cases are heard by a panel of three federal judges. After considering the evidence and arguments presented by lawyers for both sides, this panel makes one of three decisions. It says that the verdict of the original case will remain the same, it reverses that decision, or it sends the case back to a district court for a new trial. The decision of an appellate court is final unless the case is taken all the way to the Supreme Court. Taking a case to the Supreme Court is a long and complicated process, and a decision of the Supreme Court is final unless the Supreme Court itself reverses it at some later time.

Legislative Courts

Each type of legislative court was created by Congress for a specific purpose. For example, the **U.S. Claims Court** handles cases in which people or companies sue the federal government. The **U.S. Tax Court** handles cases brought by citizens who believe they are being unfairly taxed by the federal government.

Supreme Court Building, Washington, D.C.

THE U.S. SUPREME COURT

The U.S. Supreme Court is made up of nine judges, one of whom holds the title **chief justice.** Most of the Supreme Court's work consists of reviewing cases that have already been tried in lower appellate courts.

The Chosen Nine

It is a great honor to be chosen to be a Supreme Court justice, or judge. The nine justices of the Supreme Court, like all federal judges, are appointed by the president with the approval of the Senate. And, like all federal judges, they are appointed to their positions for life. The reason for appointments (rather than elections) and for lifetime terms is that judges should not feel that their jobs depend on making decisions that will be popular with the public or that will agree with the president.

On the other hand, the appointment process does allow—even encourages—presidents to make politically motivated choices. A president is apt to appoint judges who seem likely to view issues and make decisions in a way that supports the president's political ideas. (Of course, a judge is in no way obligated to act according to the president's wishes.) The Senate can refuse to approve a president's choice, but the senators must have good reasons—not just that they disagree with the person's political views.

Three Fundamental Duties

Overall, Supreme Court justices perform three important duties:

1. The foremost duty of the Court is to analyze laws and actions taken by the government to ensure that they do not violate the Constitution. This process is known as judicial review. The Court examines the laws and actions of not only the federal government but also those of local and state governments.
2. It is often necessary for the Supreme Court to give an interpretation of a law—to decide exactly what the law means and how it applies to particular circumstances.
3. The Supreme Court may <u>overturn</u> earlier decisions. Often this occurs several decades after an earlier decision, when certain judges have retired or died and the <u>ideological</u> makeup of the court has changed.

How the Court Works

The U.S. Supreme Court meets each October for a nine-month term. Each month, the justices spend two weeks hearing new cases. For each case, opposing lawyers explain their views in formal written statements called **briefs.** In a brief, a lawyer presents facts and other information relevant to the case, along with a legal argument for deciding the case in one particular way. Other people and parties with an interest in the case, such as government agencies or special interest groups, might submit their own briefs as well. After briefs have been submitted, each side's attorney delivers a thirty-minute speech in which the lawyer presents his or her view of the case as persuasively as possible. Any justice may interrupt either lawyer to ask questions or request more information.

Each Friday, the justices conduct a private conference to discuss the cases they have heard during the week. Generally, the group spends about a half hour on each case. After each justice states his or her views of the case briefly, the group takes a vote. In order for a decision to be made, a majority of the judges must agree. In the event of a tie, the court automatically **upholds,** or keeps, the previous decision by a lower court.

After two weeks of hearing cases, the court <u>recesses</u> for two weeks. During this period, each justice has time to think privately about arguments he or she has heard and prepare for upcoming trials. The justices also write **opinions,** formal written statements of their thoughts on various cases. The nine Supreme Court justices cannot write opinions for every case they decide. Still, about 150 cases end with written opinions.

Landmark Cases

Here are some of the U.S. Supreme Court's most famous decisions. Each decision is described by the names of the parties involved. The abbreviation *v.* between the two names stands for *versus,* the Latin word for "against." (For example, *Marbury v. Madison* means "Marbury against Madison.")

- Marbury v. Madison *(1803). The court ruled that it has the power to decide that an act of the president or of the legislature is unconstitutional.*
- Plessy v. Ferguson *(1896). The court ruled that it is constitutional to provide "separate but equal" public facilities for people of different races.*
- Brown v. Board of Education of Topeka *(1954). In a reversal of the fifty-year-old* Plessy v. Ferguson *decision, the court ruled that it is unconstitutional to separate the races in different public schools.*
- Gideon v. Wainwright *(1963). The court ruled that a person being tried in a state court has a right to representation by an attorney—and that the state must provide an attorney free of cost if the person cannot afford to pay for one.*
- Miranda v. Arizona *(1966). The court ruled that a person placed under arrest must be told that he or she has the right to remain silent, that he or she has the right to an attorney, and that anything he or she says may be used as evidence in court. The decision also states that nothing an accused person says before being told his or her rights can be used as evidence in court.*
- Roe v. Wade *(1973). The court ruled that it is legal under certain conditions for a woman to end a pregnancy by having an abortion.*

! *Implications*

To answer the question, "Why does all this matter?" or "What does it mean?," share the following insights with your child.

- **The process of selecting federal judges is an important example of the checks and bal-** ances that limit the powers of the executive and judicial branches of the federal government. The Constitution states that the president—"by and with the advice and consent of the Senate"—has the power and responsibility to appoint federal judges. But the required approval of the Senate checks and balances the president's power in this respect. While presidents have a degree of power over the judicial branch, they cannot simply appoint whomever they choose to a federal judgeship or a seat on the Supreme Court. At the same time, the judicial branch of the government checks and balances the legislative branch by having the power to declare a law unconstitutional.

- **Historically, Supreme Court justices have been from a similar background in terms of class, race, sex, and age.** We can assume that individual judges perform their legal duties with the utmost desire for fairness. Still, the fact that the court, over time, has been staffed by older white men from the upper classes of American society probably has not been in the best interest of promoting "equal justice under the law." The relatively recent inclusion of female and African American Supreme Court judges could mark the beginning of an era in which the court more fairly represents the diverse population of the United States of America.

- **In the United States, a person accused of a crime is considered innocent until proven guilty.** This presumption of innocence is more meaningful than it may seem on the surface. It means that, in a criminal trial, it is the responsibility of the prosecution to prove that the defendant is guilty—not the responsibility of the defense to prove that the person is innocent. In fact, all the defense attorney has to do is to show that the prosecution's argument isn't convincing enough to prove guilt beyond a **reasonable doubt.** If the prosecution can't prove the defendant's guilt, the defendant is found not guilty. This system gives an advantage to the defendant, showing that our courts bend over backward to be fair to people who are on trial.

Fact Checker

To check that your child knows or can find the basic facts in this chapter, here is a fill-in activity that requires a grasp of the structure and functioning of the judicial branch of the federal government.

Complete each sentence by filling in the blank. Each of the answers is a word that appears in boldface type and is defined in this chapter. Look back in the chapter to find any words or expressions you're not sure of.

1. All federal cases are first heard in a _____ court.

2. In a criminal case, the person accused of committing a crime is called the _____.

3. A _____ case involves a disagreement between two parties.

4. In a civil case, the two parties are called the plaintiff and the _____.

5. In a district court, criminal cases are always decided by a _____.

6. If a person thinks the decision of a district court should be reversed, he or she may take the case to an _____ court.

Answers appear in the back, preceding the index.

The Big Questions

The following questions encourage your child to think critically rather than simply recall facts. If necessary, review the specific information from the preceding pages that will help your child make the necessary inferences to come up with reasonable answers.

1. Presidential elections are considered even more important than usual when the public knows that one or more places on the Supreme Court will become vacant during the term of the candidate who wins. Why do you think that the opportunity for a president to appoint a Supreme Court justice is considered so important?

2. There are no qualifications a person must have in order to serve on a jury. In fact, most adult U.S. citizens are required by law to serve, from time to time, on a jury that will decide on the verdict in a criminal or civil trial. Why do you think ordinary citizens rather than judges or specially educated people are trusted to make such important decisions?

Suggested Answers

1. *Appointing a Supreme Court justice who agrees with the president's political ideas is a way to extend the effect a president has on the country beyond that president's term of office. The president can serve a maximum of eight years, but the justices the president appoints will serve for life.*
2. *There is no specific answer to this question. You might suggest that, in a democracy, people from all walks of life should share in this important responsibility.*

 # Skills Practice

The following activities give your child practice in applying the skills basic to social studies. For some of the activities, your child may need to review the information in the preceding pages.

A.   GIVING REASONS

Students are often asked on social studies tests to give reasons for certain facts or events. This activity will give your child practice with that skill.

Briefly explain the reason for each of the following facts. (You can find the answer to the first question in the text of this chapter. You will have to figure out the answers to the second and third questions by yourself.)

1. Federal court judges are appointed by the president and serve lifetime terms.
2. In most states, a jury's verdict in a criminal case must be unanimous.
3. If a person wants to appeal the decision of a district court, his or her case must go to an appellate court before going to the Supreme Court.

Suggested Answers

1. *Federal judges—especially justices of the Supreme Court—should not have to consider popular opinion when they make their decisions.*
2. *People convicted of crimes are often sentenced to long prison terms. If even one member of a jury doubts the accused person's guilt, the person should not be considered proven guilty beyond reasonable doubt and possibly punished unfairly.*
3. *There is only one Supreme Court. If everyone who wanted to appeal a case could go directly to the Supreme Court, there would be far too many appeals cases for the Court to hear.*

Evaluating Your Child's Skills: **In order to complete this activity successfully, your child needs to use critical thinking skills with regard to the information in this chapter. If he or she has trouble, you can**

help by asking what the result would be if the stated facts were not true. For example, "What would happen if everyone who wanted to appeal a case could go directly to the Supreme Court?

B.   MAKING A DIAGRAM

Ask your child to show visually how the system of checks and balances works with regard to the judicial branch of the federal government.

Make a diagram that shows how the relationship between the judicial branch of the federal government and the legislative and executive branches is an example of the way checks and balances work in our government. You can use whatever shapes or symbols you like to represent the three branches of the federal government. Use arrows and labels that will help to show how each branch interacts with the other.

Suggested Answers

Your child's diagram should show that the executive branch has power over the judicial branch because the president appoints federal judges; that the legislative branch has power over both the judicial and the executive branches because the Senate has to approve the president's appointments; that the judicial branch has power over the legislative because, with the power of judicial review, it can declare laws to be unconstitutional.

Evaluating Your Child's Skills: In order to complete this activity successfully, your child needs to have not only a grasp of the relationship between the three branches of government, but also the ability to represent facts visually. If he or she needs help, suggest starting with three circles in a triangular arrangement, with each circle labeled to represent one branch of the government. Then suggest drawing arrows pointing from the legislative to the executive, from the executive to the judicial, and both to and from the judicial and the legislative.

 # *Top of the Class*

Children interested in delving more deeply into the topic of this chapter can choose one or more of the following activities. They may do the activities for their own satisfaction or share what they have done in class to show that they have been seriously considering the topic of the judicial branch of the federal government.

RESEARCH: THE SUPREME COURT TODAY

Encourage your child to find out the names of the present nine Supreme Court justices, to find their pictures and be able to recognize them, and to be familiar with some of their recent decisions and opinions.

You can use the Internet to find out the names of the present nine Supreme Court justices and see their photographs. Go to Web site http://supct. law.cornell.edu/supct/justices/fullcourt.html.   From this site, you will also be able to access each justice's background and recent decisions he or she has made.

RESEARCH: HOW DO YOU GET TO THE SUPREME COURT?

This chapter does not go into how a case moves from a district court to an appellate court and all the way to the Supreme Court. That is a lengthy and complicated process, but your child might be curious to find out about it.

In a good recent edition of an encyclopedia or on the Internet, find out the path a case follows to move from a district court to an appellate court and possibly all the way to the U.S. Supreme Court. If you use the Internet, use a search engine and type in key words such as "Supreme Court,"

"U.S. legal system," or "apellate courts." You may wish to share your findings with your class.

BOOKS TO READ AND RECOMMEND IN CLASS

Suggest that your child read one or more of the following nonfiction books and respond by giving an oral or written critique in class.

Bredeson, Carmen. *Ruth Bader Ginsburg: Supreme Court Justice (People to Know* series). Enslow, 1995.

Kent, Deborah. *Thurgood Marshall and the Supreme Court (Cornerstones of Freedom* series). Children's Press, 1997.

Macht, Norman. *Sandra Day O'Connor: Supreme Court Justice (Junior World Biographies* series). Chelsea, 1992.

Stein, R. Conrad. *Powers of the Supreme Court (Cornerstones of Freedom* series). Children's Press, 1995.

CHAPTER 6

Federal Government: The Executive Branch

Executive Branch of the Federal Government

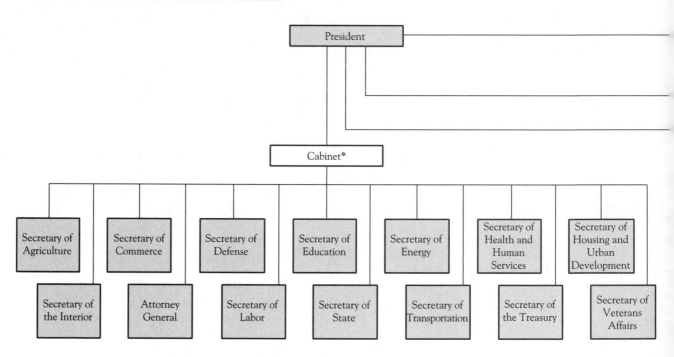

* Each member of the cabinet heads a department. For example, the Secretary of Agriculture heads the Department of Agriculture, the Attorney General heads the Department of Justice, and so on.

The executive branch of the federal government includes the president of the United States and all the departments, agencies, and individuals who work under the president. This chart shows how the executive branch of the government is organized.

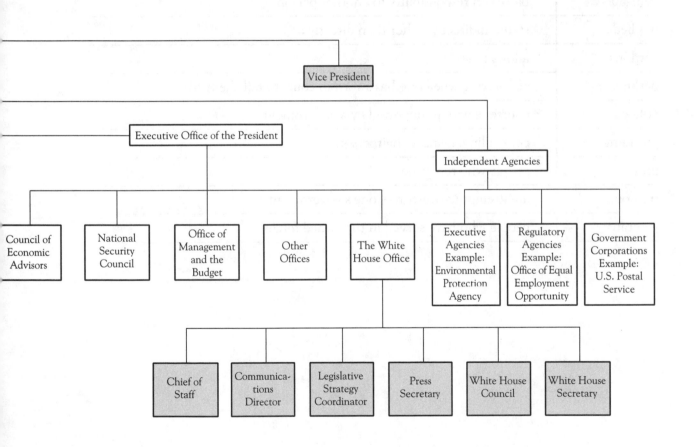

Word Power

The words on the following chart are underscored in the section called "What Your Child Needs to Know." Explain their meanings to your child either before going over the information in that section or as they come up in reading or discussion.

Word	Definition
ambassadors	people sent to foreign nations to represent their country
civilian	person who is not a member of the armed forces
delegates	passes on responsibility to another person
implied	stated indirectly rather than directly
pardons	allows to go free
perjury	act of lying when one has sworn in court to tell the truth
policy	course of action supported by a government
presiding	controlling; being a chairperson
press	people who report news
treason	an attempt to overthrow one's government
veterans	people who have served in the armed forces

What Your Child Needs to Know

You may choose to use the following text in several different ways, depending on your child's strengths and preferences. You might read the passage aloud; you might read it to yourself and then paraphrase it for your child; or you might ask your child to read the material along with you or on his or her own.

INTRODUCTION TO THE EXECUTIVE BRANCH

The executive branch of the government includes the president of the United States, the vice president, and all the other people who work for the president. In this chapter, you will see that the president has many jobs—too many for one person and just a few helpers to do. The president <u>delegates</u> important responsibilities to more than 2 million people who work for the executive branch of the government. These people include the fourteen members of the cabinet and those who work under them; the executive office of the president, which includes the president's closest advisers and personal staff; and agencies such as the U.S. Environmental Protection Agency and the U.S. Postal Service. You will also see that the president has many powers. But, while the president of the United States is the most powerful person in the country and possibly in the entire world, those powers are strictly limited by the Constitution (see Chapter 1).

THE PRESIDENT

Who can become president of the United States? To run for president, a person must be a natural-born citizen (see Chapter 2), must be at least thirty-five years old, and must have lived in the United States for at least fourteen years. A president can be male or female, can come from any race or religion, and can practice any profession, although most presidents have had experience in government and law. Once a president is elected, that person will serve for four years and can then be elected a second time for another four-year term. The only president to be elected more than twice was Franklin Delano Roosevelt—he served three terms and was elected for a fourth but died in office. Now the law limits the number of times a president can be elected to two. Early presidents were paid $25,000 a year, but the salary has been going up. Since 1999, presidents receive $400,000 a year plus $100,000 for travel expenses and $19,000 for entertaining expenses.

The President's Jobs, Duties, and Responsibilities

The president has not one, but many jobs. Following is a summary of the president's jobs and the most important duties and responsibilities that go along with each of them. The list is not complete—the president's duties are too numerous to include them all.

Chief Executive

- Sees that federal laws, judgments of federal courts, and treaties, or formal agreements with other countries, are obeyed and carried out
- Appoints federal judges, including the justices of the Supreme Court, with the approval of the majority of the Senate
- Grants <u>pardons</u> to people who have been convicted of committing federal crimes
- Sets foreign <u>policy</u> by deciding how the United States will deal with and solve problems involving foreign countries; plays an important role in world affairs

Chief Diplomat

- Appoints <u>ambassadors</u> to other countries, with the approval of the majority of the Senate
- Meets with ambassadors from foreign nations
- Helps other nations settle their disagreements
- Makes treaties with other nations, with the approval of the majority of the Senate

Commander in Chief of Armed Forces

- Orders armed forces to other places in the world in times of crisis, such as the hostage crisis in 1980, when President Jimmy Carter sent troops to Iran to try to free Americans who were being held there

- Orders armed forces to places within the United States in order to control emergency situations such as riots or floods
- Controls the use of nuclear weapons, either by ordering their use or by ordering the armed forces not to use them

Chief Legislator

- Suggests legislation
- Gives yearly State of the Union message that outlines the overall plan for legislation the president would like Congress to pass
- Tries to influence representatives to introduce legislation in Congress; tries to persuade Congress to pass or not pass legislation according to the president's plan (see Chapter 4)
- Vetoes, or refuses to sign, bills that the president does not want to become laws

Chief Economic Planner

- Prepares the federal budget, which shows how the federal government will spend money

Head of State

- Visits heads of foreign governments
- Acts as host to heads of foreign governments who visit the United States
- Conducts ceremonies such as lighting the national Christmas tree in Washington, D.C., throwing out the first baseball of the season, and dedicating parks and new government buildings

Party Leader

- Helps to shape the president's political party's ideas on issues concerning both the United States and foreign nations

The President's Powers

The president has many powers. Some of these are specifically listed in Article II, Sections 2 and 3, of the Constitution of the United States (see Chapter 1). The powers directly given to the president by the Constitution are called enumerated powers. Some of the most important of these are as follows:

- Holds the title Commander in Chief of the Armed Forces
- Appoints members of the cabinet
- Makes treaties with other countries
- Appoints judges of the Supreme Court

The enumerated powers are not the only powers exercised by the president of the United States, however. When first taking office, every president takes the Presidential Oath, which is found in the Constitution, Article II, Section 1, Clause 8.

> I do solemnly swear (or affirm) that I will faithfully execute the office of President of the United States, and will to the best of my ability, preserve, protect, and defend the Constitution of the United States.

These words can be understood to grant the president the power to do whatever is necessary to fulfill the oath, even if it means exercising powers that are not directly mentioned in the Constitution. Such powers are called implied powers. In each of the following examples, a president exercised a power that was not specifically given to him by the Constitution, but that he thought was necessary in order to "faithfully execute the office of President of the United States" or to "preserve, protect, and defend the Constitution of the United States."

- Thomas Jefferson purchased land—the Louisiana Purchase in 1803.

Portrait of Thomas Jefferson (Henry H. Robinson, 1840)

Portrait of Abraham Lincoln (Alexander Gardner, 1864)

- Abraham Lincoln issued the Emancipation Proclamation, freeing the slaves in 1863; he raised an army before he had the approval of Congress; during the Civil War he put enemies of the Union in jail without a trial.

In addition to giving many important powers to the president, the Constitution also limits presidential powers. For example, while a president can veto a bill passed by Congress (See Chapter 4), Congress can pass the bill into law over the president's veto if two-thirds of both the Senate and the House of Representatives vote to do so. The federal courts can declare a president's actions unconstitutional, as in 1974, when the Supreme Court ruled that Richard Nixon could not keep information needed in a criminal trial secret. And a president can be impeached if suspected of committing a serious crime such as bribery, treason, or perjury. To **impeach** a president, the House of Representatives identifies the charges against the president, and the majority of the representatives vote to accept the charges. A president who has been impeached is then tried by the Senate and removed from office only if two-thirds of the Senators agree to do so. The only two presidents who have been impeached are Andrew Johnson and Bill Clinton, but neither one was removed from office. The Constitution also limits presidential power by listing things the president may not do at all, such as declaring war (see Chapter 4) and making laws, and things the president can do only with the approval of Congress, such as appointing Supreme Court justices and making treaties with foreign nations.

THE VICE PRESIDENT

The vice president's most important duty is to be ready to take over the presidency if the president dies or is removed from office and to become *acting president* if the president is temporarily unable to fulfill duties because of an accident or illness. Another of the vice president's duties is presiding over the Senate without taking part in any lawmaking activities. The vice president calls on senators who wish to speak, as a teacher calls on students who raise their hands in class. Usually the **president pro tempore** of the Senate—a member of the majority party—takes over the job of presiding over the Senate, however. In case there is a tied vote in the Senate, the vice president may break the tie by casting the deciding vote.

The president really decides how active in government the vice president will be. For example, Franklin Delano Roosevelt gave little responsibility to his vice president, Harry Truman. President Clinton, on the other hand, encouraged Al Gore to be extremely active as vice president.

If the vice president dies, the president nominates someone else to fill that position. The nomination must then be approved by Congress.

THE CABINET AND EXECUTIVE DEPARTMENTS

In government, a **cabinet** consists of a group of advisers to the head of a government. The cabinet of the United States includes the vice president and the heads of the fourteen **executive departments.** The head of each department has a staff of people whom he or she supervises. The department heads are appointed by the president, but each one must be confirmed, or approved, by two-thirds of the Senate.

Following is a list of the fourteen executive departments with a brief description of each one's most important purposes.

- The **Department of Agriculture (USDA)** is headed by the secretary of agriculture. It aids farmers by helping them conserve soil and water and by conducting research on how to grow better crops. It inspects meat and vegetables for nutritional value and quality and advises the public about nutrition. It also provides food stamps to help needy people buy food and helps other nations improve food production.

- The **Department of Commerce** is headed by the secretary of commerce. It helps the nation advance economically and technologically. It provides information and advice to private businesses. It issues patents and trademarks to people who create new products so that other people cannot steal their ideas. It conducts the **census,** or population count, that asks people questions about the way they live in order to provide the government with important information and statistics about the population of the United States.

- The **Department of Defense (DOD)** is headed by the secretary of defense. It is responsible for the nation's armed forces—the Army, Navy, Air Force, and Marines. The secretary of defense does not belong to any of the armed forces, but the department includes the Joint Chiefs of Staff, which consists of a chairperson and the chiefs of the Army, Navy, and Air Force and the commandant of the Marine Corps. Members of the Joint Chiefs of Staff are the president's main military advisers.

- The **Department of Education** is headed by the secretary of education. It gives states money to help improve schools, provides financial aid for students, and conducts research to improve the quality of education in the nation's classrooms.

- The **Department of Energy (DOE)** is headed by the secretary of energy. It conducts research on how to improve the quality of the environment and how to best use and manage natural resources.

- The **Department of Health and Human Services (HHS)** is headed by the secretary of health and human services. It helps protect the health of the American people. It includes the Centers for Disease Control and Prevention, which sets safety and health standards for workers. It also includes the Food and Drug Administration, which enforces laws designed to ensure the purity, effectiveness, and truthful labeling of food and medicines.

- The **Department of Housing and Urban Development (HUD)** is headed by the secretary of housing and urban development. It helps people get loans to buy houses, makes sure that people are able to find housing without being discriminated against, and helps homeless people to find places to live.

- The **Department of the Interior** is headed by the secretary of the interior. It supervises the nation's natural resources, including minerals, water, fish, and wildlife. It helps acquire recreation and parklands for federal, state, and local governments. It includes the National Park Service.

- The **Department of Justice (DOJ)** is headed by the attorney general of the United States. It investigates people and institutions suspected of breaking federal laws. It includes the Criminal Division, Bureau of Prisons, Civil Rights Division, Tax Division, Drug Enforcement Administration, Federal Bureau of Investigation (FBI), and other divisions.

- The **Department of Labor** is headed by the secretary of labor. It helps improve people's working conditions and opportunities for employment. It helps prevent job discrimination and unfair treatment of children who have jobs, and it makes sure that people are not paid lower wages than are required by law.

- The **Department of State** is headed by the secretary of state. It helps plan how the United States will deal with governments of other countries. It helps U.S. citizens living and traveling in other countries. It helps decide which foreign nations the United States should give or lend money to.

- The **Department of Transportation (DOT)** is headed by the secretary of transportation. It helps to make sure that Americans have good and safe transportation systems. Among other offices, it includes the Urban Mass Transportation Administration, which helps cities provide public transportation such as buses and subways.

- The **Department of the Treasury** is headed by the secretary of the treasury. It makes paper money and coins, collects taxes, and controls banks. The Secret Service is part of this department because it was originally set up to guard against counterfeiting. Now the Secret Service protects the president and other important people in government.

- The **Department of Veterans' Affairs** is headed by the secretary of veterans' affairs. It makes sure that veterans get the medical care and other help to which they and their families are entitled by law.

THE EXECUTIVE OFFICE OF THE PRESIDENT (EOP)

The Executive Office of the President is made up of individuals and agencies that directly assist the president. Some of the most important agencies are listed here.

- The **Council of Economic Advisers** includes three top economists, with about sixty more economists working under them. It also includes lawyers and political experts. The Council of Economic Advisers helps control the

nation's economy by proposing solutions to problems such as unemployment.

- The **National Security Council** is headed by the president. Other main members include the vice president, the secretary of defense, the secretary of state, the chairperson of the Joint Chiefs of Staff, and the director of the Central Intelligence Agency (CIA).
- The **Office of Management and Budget (OMB)** helps to decide which programs the federal government will pay for and how much it will spend.
- The **White House Office** consists of a staff of people appointed by the president without approval by the Senate. The people who work for the White House Office gather information and give advice about important issues and problems facing the president. They are the president's close advisers and personal staff—the only people who often see and meet directly with the president. The following chart shows the most important individuals who work for the White House Office and what their responsibilities are.

THE WHITE HOUSE OFFICE

Individual's Title	Responsibilities
Chief of staff	Meets with the president several times a day to discuss policies and ideas; recommends people the president should meet with; communicates with and directs the work of people on the president's staff; meets with members of Congress to influence them to support the president's ideas
Communications director	Directs a staff who write speeches for the president and prepare statements about the president's policies
Legislative strategy coordinator	Helps the president plan legislation to be suggested to Congress
Press secretary	Presents the president's views to the outside world; meets with news reporters each day to answer their questions and tell them what the president is doing that day; helps the president get ready for conferences with the press; prepares press releases, or written information for reporters, about the president's activities
White House counsel	As the president's lawyer, advises the president on whether or not a decision or things that happen as a result of that decision will cause legal problems
White House secretary	Keeps track of the president's appointments and daily activities; helps the president keep track of telephone calls and letters that must be answered

THE INDEPENDENT AGENCIES

In addition to the executive departments and the Executive Office of the President, there are more than two hundred independent agencies in the executive branch of the federal government—too many to list and describe here. The independent agencies fall into three categories:

- The **executive agencies** include the U.S. Environmental Protection Agency, which protects the environment from pollution. It helps the Office of Environmental Policy (part of the Executive Office of the President) to find ways to protect the environment and recommend them to the president.
- The **regulatory commissions** include the Equal Employment Opportunity Commission, which protects against job discrimination.
- The **government corporations** include the U.S. Postal Service.

 # Implications

> To answer the question, "Why does all this matter?" or "What does it mean?," share the following insights with your child.

If you think about all the details you've learned about the executive branch of the government and then ask yourself the question, "What does all this say about the United States of America as a country?," you can learn even more. Let's ask that question as we look at a few details mentioned in this chapter.

- **The president's salary is $400,000 a year.** That sounds like a pretty good salary. But the wealthiest people in the country make much more. And don't forget that the president is the highest-paid person in our government—

others, including the attorney general and the secretary of state, make less money. From these facts, we can assume that people who work in the executive branch do so for reasons other than money. For some, the reason may be desire for fame or power, but for many, it is the desire to serve their country.

- **The president is commander in chief of the Armed Forces.** The final authority on military matters, including important ones like the use of weapons, rests with the president, who is not a member of the military. In other words, the armed forces may not act unless under orders by a <u>civilian</u>. This policy means that, while the United States maintains armed forces to defend our country if necessary, it is not primarily a military nation.
- **The president cannot make laws.** As chief legislator, the president guides the legislation that Congress will pass, but the president cannot actually make laws or even introduce a bill in Congress. The president's staff may meet with legislators, write them letters, or talk to them on the telephone to try to influence or persuade them to introduce or support a bill. This system requires that the president and other members of the executive branch be good at arguing logically and using persuasive writing and speaking skills. They must also have good communication with members of Congress and keep up good relationships with them.
- **The president acts as both chief executive and head of state.** In many countries, the chief executive is a president or prime minister who is elected to office. But the head of state—the person who performs ceremonial duties and is the symbol of the country—is a king or queen, who is not elected to office, but inherits the throne. In the United States, the person who symbolizes our country and what it stands for is the president—an official elected by the people.

Fact Checker

To check that your child knows or can find the basic facts in this chapter, here is a puzzle using facts about the executive branch of the government.

PRESIDENT PUZZLE

Answer the questions by filling in the blanks, one letter to a blank. Then copy each numbered letter in your answers onto the corresponding numbered blank at the bottom of the puzzle. You will spell out one of the president's many jobs.

The president may __ __ __ __ __ __ a person convicted of a federal crime.
                            4

A president must be __ __ __ __ __ __ __ __ __ before being removed from office.
                               1

The __ __ __ __ __ secretary keeps reporters informed about the president.
          2

The secretary of state is a member of the __ __ __ __ __ __ __.
                                    8

The president can __ __ __ __ a bill passed by Congress to prevent it from becoming a law.
                10

A president may be elected a maximum of __ __ __ times.
                                   5

The president makes __ __ __ __ __ __ __ __ __, or agreements, with foreign countries.
                9

The powers that are not directly given to the president by the Constitution are called __ __ __ __ __ __ __ powers.
                11

Only the president can order the use of nuclear __ __ __ __ __ __.
                                3

To run for president, a person must live in the United States for at least __ __ __ __ __ __ __ __ years.
 6

A president needs the approval of the __ __ __ __ __ __ to appoint a justice of the Supreme Court.
                               7

__ __ __ __ __ __ __ __ __ __ __
1 2 3 4 5 6 7 8 9 10 11

Answers appear in the back, preceding the index.

? The Big Questions

The following questions encourage your child to think critically rather than simply recall facts. If necessary, review the specific information from the preceding pages that will help your child make the necessary inferences to come up with reasonable answers.

1. What requirements must someone fulfill to be nominated and to run for president? What reasons can you think of for these requirements?
2. It seems that the vice president does not have many powers or responsibilities. Why does the executive branch of the government need a vice president?
3. The position of White House press secretary is considered very important. Why do you think this is so?
4. Why do you think a president may be elected to only two terms in office?

Suggested Answers

1. A person younger than thirty-five may not be mature enough or have enough experience to carry out the many duties and responsibilities of the president; a person who is not a natural-born citizen of the United States may have loyalties to another country; a person who has lived in the United States less than fourteen years may not have enough knowledge or experience of life in this country to understand all the country's problems and needs.
2. Without a vice president, if the president died or became temporarily disabled, new elections would have to be held. A long time would pass with no one to fulfill the president's many duties and responsibilities. Having a vice president ensures that the country will continue to run smoothly, no matter what happens.
3. Since the president is elected by the people, the people of the United States have a right to know of the president's activities. The way people find out about the president's activities is through the news media. And the press secretary is the person responsible for keeping news reporters informed of the president's daily activities.
4. A president who served twelve or more years in office could become too powerful.

Skills Practice

The following activities give your child practice in applying the skills basic to social studies. For some of the activities, your child may need to review the information in the preceding pages.

A. READING A CHART

With your child, look at the chart at the beginning of this chapter, and ask him or her the following questions.

1. Who is the head of the executive branch of the U.S. government?
2. What are the four divisions of the executive branch under the president?
3. The White House Office Staff is a part of which division of the executive branch?
4. Of which executive department is the attorney general the head?

Answers

1. The president
2. The vice president, the cabinet and the executive departments, the Executive Office of the President, the independent agencies
3. The Executive Office of the President
4. The Department of Justice

Evaluating Your Child's Skills: In order to complete this activity successfully, your child will need to interpret and extract information from a graphic representation by focusing on a variety of details. If your child needs help with any of the answers, isolate for him or her the part of the chart to focus on.

B. DISTINGUISHING FACT FROM OPINION

Review with your child the definitions of the words *fact* and *opinion*. Establish that statements of facts can be checked to find out whether they are true or false, while statements of opinion are neither true nor false. Then ask your child to identify the following statements as facts or opinions. Encourage your child to explain each identification.

1. The president serves as both chief executive and head of state.
2. The president should not be allowed to serve for more than two terms.
3. The White House Chief of Staff is the most important person under the president.
4. The president should be able to appoint cabinet members without the approval of Congress.
5. The U.S. Postal Service is one of the independent agencies of the executive branch.

Answers

1. *Fact*
2. *Opinion*
3. *Opinion*
4. *Opinion*
5. *Fact*

Evaluating Your Child's Skills: In order to complete this activity successfully, your child needs to understand the difference between fact and opinion. If your child has trouble, give him or her some simple examples of facts and opinions from everyday life, for example:

Fact: "You are in the fourth grade now."

Opinion: "Dogs are better pets than cats."

Opinion: "Everyone should learn how to cook."

Alert your child to examples of key words that signal opinions: *better, should, more important.*

C. SUPPORTING AN OPINION WITH REASONS

Make sure your child understands that when a person states an opinion someone else may disagree with it. Therefore, people who state opinions should be prepared to support them, or back them up, with reasons or logical arguments. Ask your child to choose one of the following opinions and support it with at least one reason.

1. The president of the United States should/should not be able to declare war on another country.
2. Congress should/should not be able to impeach the president.

Possible Answers

1. Should: *Sometimes action may have to be taken too quickly to get Congress's approval.* Should not: *War is too important an issue to be decided on by one person, even if that person is the president.*
2. Should: *A president who commits a major crime should be removed from office.* Should not: *Members of Congress who dislike or disagree with the president can make false charges to weaken the president's power.*

Evaluating Your Child's Skills: In order to complete this activity successfully, your child needs to use analytical and logical thinking skills. If he or she has trouble, have him or her practice by backing up opinions about more familiar issues, for example:

Everyone should/should not learn how to cook.

Should: Eating is necessary for survival, and everyone should be able to survive on his or her own.

Should not: Some people do not enjoy cooking and are not good at it. Instead of spending time cooking, these people could be doing things they like to do and do well.

Top of the Class

Children interested in delving more deeply into the topic of this chapter can choose one or more of the following activities. They may do the activities for their own satisfaction or share what they have done in class to show that they have been seriously considering the topic of the executive branch of the federal government.

A POINT TO PONDER

Suggest to your child that he or she raise the following issue in class.

A *bureaucracy* is defined as "a body of officials and administrators, especially in a government" and also as "excessive multiplication of, and concentration of power in, bureaus [offices] or administrators," and "administration characterized by excessive red tape and routine." With more than 2 million people working in the executive branch of the government, is government in danger of becoming too big and bureaucratic? How can the president, the cabinet, and the White House staff keep track of what is going on in all the offices and agencies and manage the activities of so many people?

BOOKS TO READ

Suggest that your child read one or more of the following nonfiction books and respond to it by offering an oral or written critique in class.

Feinberg, Barbara S. *The Cabinet.* Twenty-First Century, 1995.
Patrick, Diane. *The Executive Branch.* Watts, 1995.
Sandler, Martin W. *Presidents.* HarperCollins, 2001.
Spies, Karen B. *Our Presidency.* Millbrook, 1994.

THE PRESIDENT IN ACTION: SEE IT ON TV

Invite your child to watch a TV show that relates to the executive branch. He or she may want to raise issues in class that come up on the show.

The popular television series *The West Wing* presents a fictional but fast-paced and exciting picture of life in the West Wing of the White House, where the president's Oval Office is located and where he works with members of the White House office staff. Children will be able to identify the main characters who play the president, chief of staff, White House counsel, press secretary, legislative strategy coordinator, communications director, and White House secretary.

WEB SITES TO EXPLORE

Children can use the Internet to find further information about the topic of this chapter. They can share the Web sites they discover with their classmates and teacher.

By typing in the key words "White House" or "President of the United States," your child can use a search engine to find Web sites that provide in-depth information about the executive branch of the federal government—for example, the White House Official Site, The White House for Kids, Executive Branch Federal Agencies, White House News, and Executive Branch Television, which provides coverage of agency hearings and White House briefings.

CHAPTER 7
Policy

This illustration provides an overview of various types of policy generated by the U.S. government.

Foreign Policy

Europe

Asia

South America

Africa

Central America

Education

Housing

Health

Transportation

Agriculture

Business & Labor

Public Assistance

Environment

U.S. Government Policy

Word Power

The words on the following chart are underscored in the section called "What Your Child Needs to Know." Explain their meanings to your child as needed when they come up in reading or discussion. Keep the list handy for you and your child to use.

Word	Definition
domestic	regarding the home
exploiting	treating unfairly
forecasts	predicts
management	employers, business that employs workers
negotiate	bargain, deal
regulate	control or manage
stimulates	helps, activates
strike	stop work in order to force an employer to meet demands of workers
toxins	poisonous substances
violated	not respected

What Your Child Needs to Know

You may choose to use the following text in several different ways, depending on your child's strengths and preferences. You might read the passage aloud; you might read it to yourself and then paraphrase it for your child; or you might ask you child to read the material along with you or on his or her own.

INTRODUCTION TO POLICY

The word *policy* means a general plan or method that governs specific actions. For example, if you want to return an item to a store, the manager might tell you, "You can make an exchange, but it's not our policy to give cash refunds." The manager would mean that the store has a general rule against giving refunds and therefore, you, as an individual, will not be able to get your money back.

Governments also have policies, or general plans, that determine how they handle issues and conditions within their own countries and how they respond to conditions and issues in foreign countries around the world. The term **domestic** policy refers to our nation's policies regarding situations within the United States. The term **foreign policy** refers to our nation's policies with regard to foreign countries. This chapter explains how the federal government sets policy.

DOMESTIC POLICY

The basic goal of domestic policy is to preserve and improve the quality of life for citizens of the United States. Specific policies may change, but the goal is always the same no matter who the president is and no matter which political party is in power. The federal government determines domestic policy by choosing which issues need attention and by deciding how to spend available money on those issues.

The number and range of policy issues is dizzying. It might help to divide these issues into five basic categories: business and labor, agriculture, the environment, transportation, and social policy—policy focused more directly on people.

Business and Labor

The U.S. government supports business within the country and also promotes the sale of American products around the world. The federal government **stimulates** business in several ways.

One way is by encouraging companies to start up or expand by allowing them to pay less money in taxes. Also, the government lends money to companies—especially to small businesses—as a way of helping them establish themselves in the marketplace. Finally, the government occasionally gives money to help businesses that are considered necessary to the well-being of the people living in a community. Such businesses might include a bus or ferryboat company.

In order to meet its goal of preserving and improving the quality of life for U.S. citizens, it is important for the government not only to stimulate but also to **regulate** businesses. Government regulation of business ensures good working conditions for workers and prevents **management** from **exploiting** them. For instance, since the 1930s, many employers in the United States have had to pay a **minimum wage** that is set by either a state government or the federal government. In addition to managing wages, Congress has passed laws limiting the number of hours an employee can be required to work. Other laws restrict the use of children as laborers and spell out how employers must provide a healthy, safe workplace for employees.

Also in the interest of protecting workers from being exploited by management, the federal government has introduced and passed laws supporting the activities of **labor unions**—groups of workers who have joined together to make sure they are treated fairly. Unions enable workers to **negotiate** as a group with employers, as well as the right to **strike** in order to force management to give them fair wages and acceptable working conditions. The government tries to balance the rights of laborers with the rights of business owners.

Agriculture

Agriculture, or farming, provides the people of the United States with the most important necessity of life—food. Through the U.S. Department of Agriculture, the federal government supports and promotes American farmers and their crops.

One of the tasks of the Department of Agriculture is to help farmers know which crops they will be able to sell. For example, the government <u>forecasts</u> the need for various crops and then helps farmers plan which crops to plant and in what amounts. Another important aim of federal agriculture policy is to make sure that farmers are paid well for their crops. To do this, the government employs a few strategies.

- First, it lends money to farmers to help them grow a particular crop. If the price of that crop drops below a certain amount set by the government, the farmer can pay off the loan with the crop itself rather than with money.
- The federal government tells farmers how much land they can use to grow certain crops. This prevents farmers from producing too much of a certain crop and then being unable to sell it.

The Environment

For the past several decades, the U.S. government has developed policy to protect and reclaim the nation's **environment**—that is, its land, air, and water. Before it seized the attention of world leaders in the late 1940s, the condition of the environment—not only in America but worldwide—had reached a state of crisis. Finally, Congress began to write and pass laws designed to stop industries from sending <u>toxins</u> into the air and to stop factories, cities, and farmers from pouring chemicals into the nation's waterways. Other laws sought to find ways to clean up the mess that had already been made of the environment. The federal government made its first significant strides in the 1960s and 1970s, passing two clean air acts: the Air Quality Control Act and the Water Quality Improvement Act. By the 1990s, the federal government's environmental policy had even forced automobile makers to redesign engines so that cars would emit less pollution into the air.

Transportation

After the invention of the automobile, the federal government created policy to provide money for building more and more roads. Eventually, it developed a system of highways to connect states and major cities. The **Federal Highway Administration** supervises all federal roads. Most important, it gives money to states to build and improve the highways that connect that nation's major cities. In addition, the **Urban Mass Transit Administration (UMTA)** gives money to cities to help them build better public transportation systems. Better **mass transit** helps reduce the heavy traffic problem that exists in many cities.

The government also supports and regulates other types of transportation. The **Federal Aviation Administration** and the **Federal Railroad Administration** oversee air and rail travel, for example. These agencies set safety standards and also set minimum and maximum rates that transportation companies can charge passengers.

Social Policy: Education

The federal government creates policy that affects public education across the United States. In this country, public education includes elementary, middle, and secondary schools as well as public colleges and universities. All of these are run according to state guidelines and regulations. However, public schools for students in kindergarten through grade twelve are largely controlled by local government.

How does the federal government affect public schools? Primarily, it does so with money. Congress sets aside nearly $30 billion each year to be used for public schools and universities. Some of this money can be used to buy new textbooks, pay teachers' salaries, or build new classrooms, libraries, and playgrounds. Other funds may be designated for more specific purposes, such as teaching government and citizenship in middle schools. In this way, the federal government can have a significant effect on what and how children learn.

Social Policy: Public Assistance, Health, and Housing

The federal government provides services for many citizens, including people who are elderly, unemployed, poor, ill, or disabled.

The U.S. government helps people with employment or health problems through three **social insurance** programs. Each is designed to encourage the financial security of U.S. citizens.

1. The federal government takes a small amount of money from each employee's paycheck and the employer who issues the check. This money is sent to the **Social Security Administration** and set aside until the employee reaches age sixty-two. Then the money is given back to the employee during the years that follow—a period when most Americans are less able to work and earn a living than when they were younger.
2. The same basic system is used to provide **Medicare** services for senior citizens. This money is given back to senior citizens to ensure that they will be able to pay for medicine, office visits to doctors, the cost of hospitalization, and so on.
3. The federal government taxes employers to provide funds for **unemployment insurance** for workers who lose their jobs. The federal government sends this money to state agencies that then deliver the money to workers while they look for new work.

In addition to funding social insurance programs, the federal government provides money for several **public assistance** programs that aid poor people.

1. Families in which the primary wage earner has died, been disabled, or left the family can be eligible for **Aid to Families with Dependent Children** if their income level is low enough.
2. Started more than forty years ago as a way for approximately 350,000 poor people to increase their ability to buy food, the **food stamps** program has ballooned to the point that 23 million Americans use the stamps to supplement their own incomes.
3. **Medicaid** is a federal program that helps poor people pay medical bills.
4. The U.S. government is responsible also for promoting and maintaining **public health.** This happens primarily through the Medicare and Medicaid programs. In addition, the federal government provides health care for veterans and conducts research on health and medical subjects through the U.S. Department of Health and Human Services (HHS). One division of HHS, the **Food and Drug Admin-**

istration, concerns itself with testing food and drugs to ensure that they are safe for people.
5. The U.S. government takes an active role in helping citizens buy, build, or rent housing. For example, the **Federal Housing Administration (FHA)** helps people get loans to buy houses and provides public housing for which people may pay affordable rents. However promising this strategy seems in theory, it has proved challenging in reality. For decades, the majority of public housing projects have been plagued by an array of social problems, including crime, vandalism, and mismanagement. These problems show how difficult it can be for government to try to solve complicated social problems.

FOREIGN POLICY

As the goal of domestic policy is to make life in the United States as comfortable, healthy, secure, and prosperous as possible, foreign policy also has one main goal. That goal is to ensure our national security. While other goals also influence the nation's policies and actions toward other countries, they usually contribute to this one main goal. For example, the United States tries to help maintain world peace. This is a worthy goal in itself, yet the main reason for attempting to attain this goal is that, in a peaceful world, there is less chance that the United States will be drawn into a dangerous international conflict. The United States promotes national security by building and maintaining strong economic, cultural, and military relationships with other nations around the globe. Specifically, this includes signing peace treaties and other agreements, sending diplomats to other countries, organizing **summit** meetings with heads of state from different countries, and sometimes even sending military troops to other countries or declaring war. The United States also offers **foreign aid** to other countries. The aid may take the form of loans to be used for building roads, schools, and hospitals, or it may include helping a nation torn by war to rebuild, as the United States did with Japan and Germany after World War II.

Following is a list of other foreign policy goals. All of these contribute to the main goal, national security.

- **Free trade** is an important foreign policy goal that is closely related to national security. The United States supports the idea that trading goods and services with other nations benefits Americans as well as people in other countries. For example, the United States produces so much corn, cotton, and computer software that Americans could not possibly use all of it. We need to **export,** or sell in other countries, some of the goods we produce. Likewise, our government **imports,** or brings in, goods from many foreign nations. For instance, the United States does not produce enough oil for all our fuel needs, so it imports oil from several Middle Eastern nations. Some goods, such as shoes and clothing made in the United States, are very expensive because materials and workers' wages are more costly here than in other countries. Therefore, the United States imports some goods from other countries so that they can be sold more cheaply here. A movement to support American labor by buying American goods is often in conflict with being able to provide American consumers with goods they can afford to buy.
- **Supporting other democratic governments around the world** is another fundamental aim of American foreign policy. The United States lends money, military equipment, or soldiers to help democratic nations involved in military conflicts. The United States also gives financial aid to help developing nations establish stable democratic governments.
- **Human rights** around the globe are supported by the U.S. government. Along with the governments of many other nations, the U.S. government tries to identify and respond quickly to situations in which human beings' basic rights are <u>violated</u> by another government. Sometimes the offending government will stop the unacceptable actions when pressure is applied by other nations. One common method of pressuring foreign governments is to threaten to stop trading with them.

The Role of the Executive Branch

The executive branch has a great deal of power to make foreign policy. In addition to the president, the president's advisers—in particular, the secre-

President Bill Clinton with Joint Chiefs of Staff

tary of state, the secretary of defense, and the national security adviser—play a crucial part in forming foreign policy. Here are some of the ways the executive branch influences foreign policy.

- As commander in chief of the U.S. military forces, the president can order the army to invade another country.
- The president appoints **ambassadors** to nations around the globe. These diplomats work daily with ambassadors of other nations to develop cooperation among their countries.
- The president has the power to make treaties with other nations.
- The president takes the role of America's symbolic leader in meetings, gatherings, and ceremonies around the world.

The Role of Congress

The U.S. Congress has the power to declare war and the power to make decisions about how money will be spent. Although the president can order troops into a foreign country without a formal declaration of war (see Chapter 4), only Congress can appropriate money for weapons and military operations. Therefore, the legislature has a strong influence on foreign affairs. For example, if a president orders a military attack and enough senators and representatives disagree with that action, Congress could refuse to provide the funds necessary to keep the attack going over time.

Another way Congress controls foreign policy is through its power to ratify treaties with foreign nations. Two-thirds of the legislature must vote to ratify any treaty made by the president.

Implications

> To answer the question, "Why does all this matter?" or "What does it mean?," share the following insights with your child.

- By **creating policy and then putting it into practice, the federal government shapes American society in profound ways.** Nearly every aspect of modern life, including the food we eat, the products we buy, the way we travel, and the subjects taught in our schools, is influenced by domestic or foreign policy decisions made in Washington, D.C.

- **Citizens of the United States can have a powerful influence on American foreign policy.** During the late 1960s, for example, Americans began to question—and then to protest—our nation's involvement in the Vietnam War. Anti-war demonstrations grew larger and more bitter, influencing President Lyndon Johnson's decision not to run for reelection and President Richard Nixon's eventual decision to withdraw American military forces from Southeast Asia.

 Fact Checker

> To check that your child knows or can find the basic facts in this chapter, here is a puzzle based on information discussed.

Across

2. The _____ is the main person responsible for setting foreign policy.

5. _____ policy relates to conditions within the United States.

7. Sometimes the United States gives economic _____ to help other nations.

8. The most important goal of foreign policy is national _____.

9. _____ policy involves other countries.

Down

1. The purpose of _____ is to provide older citizens with medical care they can afford.

3. One reason for _____ with other countries is to provide markets for U.S. products.

4. Another word for "control" is _____.

6. The president signs _____, or makes agreements, with other countries.

Answers appear in the back, preceding the index.

? The Big Questions

The following questions encourage your child to think critically rather than simply recall facts. If necessary, review the specific information from the preceding pages that will help your child make the appropriate inferences to come up with reasonable answers.

1. Some people think the government can go too far with policies that regulate, or limit, business. For example, in an effort to protect the environment, the government has required automobile manufacturers to include safety features in their cars, as well as features that decrease air pollution caused by the fuel that cars burn. These regulations cost the automobile industry money and, in turn, drive up the cost of cars. Are you in favor of or against government regulation of business? What are your reasons for your opinion?

2. One way the U.S. government can try to influence other countries to improve their human rights records is by refusing to trade with countries that deny basic human rights to their citizens. Some people have criticized the United States for appointing itself watchdog over other countries' practices. What is your opinion on this matter? Is it our responsibility to discourage lack of respect for human rights around the world, or is the way other countries treat their citizens none of our business?

Answers

1. *Accept any answers that are supported with sound reasoning.*
2. *Accept any answers that are supported with sound reasoning.*

Skills Practice

The following activities give your child practice in applying the skills basic to social studies. For some of the activities, your child may need to review the information in the preceding pages.

A. APPLYING GENERAL PRINCIPLES TO NEW SITUATIONS

Being able to think about a general principle and apply it to a new situation is a true test of your child's understanding of the principle.

Imagine that a war has broken out between two countries in another part of the world. Briefly describe how the U.S. government might respond in both of the following situations.

1. Assume that the U.S. government is pursuing a foreign policy of internationalism.
2. Assume that the U.S. government is pursuing a foreign policy of isolationism.

Suggested Answers

1. *Your child's answer should include the U.S. government's getting involved in some way—*
perhaps by organizing peace talks between the two countries or even by becoming militarily involved.
2. *Under a policy of isolationism, the United States would remain uninvolved.*

Evaluating Your Child's Skills: **In order to complete this activity successfully, your child needs to understand the two opposite types of foreign policy and to apply that understanding to a possible future situation.**

B. DISTINGUISHING MAIN IDEAS FROM DETAILS

Being able to zero in on the main idea of a paragraph is an important skill in social studies and all the curriculum areas.

Read the following two paragraphs that contain information from this chapter. State the main idea in each. Remember that a detail in a paragraph can be important without being the main idea of that paragraph. Also remember that the main idea is not always the first sentence in a paragraph.

1. The U.S. government sometimes allows companies to pay less money in taxes. It lends money to help establish small businesses. It occasionally even gives money to businesses that are essential to the well-being of the people living in a community—for example, a company that provides public transportation. The federal government uses these and other methods to support and promote business.

2. The main goal of U.S. foreign policy is to ensure the national security, and all other goals are secondary. Supporting other democratic nations, giving financial aid to developing nations, and promoting world peace, in the long run, are all in the interest of national security. Of course, these are worthy goals in themselves as well.

Answers

1. *The federal government uses these and other methods to support and promote business.*
2. *The main goal of U.S. foreign policy is to ensure the national security, and all other goals are secondary.*

Evaluating Your Child's Skills: In order to complete this activity successfully, your child needs to understand the difference between the main idea of a paragraph and the details that support that idea. If he or she has trouble, help your child to see that the main-idea sentence in each paragraph is the one that is supported by the other sentences—that is, the other sentences show that the main-idea sentence is true.

Top of the Class

Children interested in delving more deeply into the topics covered in this chapter can choose one or more of the following activities. They may do the activities for their own satisfaction or report in class on what they have done to show that they have been seriously considering U.S. domestic and foreign policy.

A POINT TO PONDER

Suggest to your child that he or she raise the following issue for discussion in class.

Just how influential *is* the United States in world affairs? If the U.S. government were to stay out of other countries' business (the foreign policy the United States held to earlier in its history), how might current situations in the world be affected? For examples, look through current newspapers for situations abroad over which the United States has influence.

BOOK TO READ AND RECOMMEND IN CLASS

Suggest that your child read the following nonfiction book and respond to it by giving an oral or written critique in class.

Spies, Karen B. *Isolation vs. Intervention: Is America the World's Police Force?* (Issues of Our Time series). Twenty-First Century, 1995.

CHAPTER 8

Taxing and Spending

Form **1040**	Department of the Treasury—Internal Revenue Service **U.S. Individual Income Tax Return** **2001**	(99)	IRS Use Only—Do not write or staple in this space.

For the year Jan. 1–Dec. 31, 2001, or other tax year beginning _____ , 2001, ending _____ 20 _____ | OMB No. 1545-0074

Label
(See instructions on page 19.)

Use the IRS label. Otherwise, please print or type.

L A B E L   H E R E

Your first name and initial — Last name — Your social security number

If a joint return, spouse's first name and initial — Last name — Spouse's social security number

Home address (number and street). If you have a P.O. box, see page 19. — Apt. no.

City, town or post office, state, and ZIP code. If you have a foreign address, see page 19.

▲ **Important!** ▲
You **must** enter your SSN(s) above.

Presidential Election Campaign (See page 19.)

Note. Checking "Yes" will not change your tax or reduce your refund.
Do you, or your spouse if filing a joint return, want $3 to go to this fund? . . . . ▶

You: ☐ Yes ☐ No   Spouse: ☐ Yes ☐ No

Filing Status

Check only one box.

1 ☐ Single
2 ☐ Married filing joint return (even if only one had income)
3 ☐ Married filing separate return. Enter spouse's social security no. above and full name here. ▶ _____
4 ☐ Head of household (with qualifying person). (See page 19.) If the qualifying person is a child but not your dependent, enter this child's name here. ▶ _____
5 ☐ Qualifying widow(er) with dependent child (year spouse died ▶ _____). (See page 19.)

Exemptions

6a ☐ **Yourself.** If your parent (or someone else) can claim you as a dependent on his or her tax return, **do not** check box 6a . . . .

b ☐ **Spouse** . . . .

c **Dependents:**

(1) First name — Last name	(2) Dependent's social security number	(3) Dependent's relationship to you	(4) ✓ If qualifying child for child tax credit (see page 20)
			☐
			☐
			☐
			☐
			☐
			☐

If more than six dependents, see page 20.

No. of boxes checked on 6a and 6b _____
No. of your children on 6c who:
• lived with you _____
• did not live with you due to divorce or separation (see page 20) _____
Dependents on 6c not entered above _____
Add numbers entered on lines above ▶ _____

d Total number of exemptions claimed . . . .

Income

Attach Forms W-2 and W-2G here. Also attach Form(s) 1099-R if tax was withheld.

If you did not get a W-2, see page 21.

Enclose, but do not attach, any payment. Also, please use Form 1040-V.

7	Wages, salaries, tips, etc. Attach Form(s) W-2	7
8a	**Taxable** interest. Attach Schedule B if required	8a
b	**Tax-exempt** interest. **Do not** include on line 8a	8b
9	Ordinary dividends. Attach Schedule B if required	9
10	Taxable refunds, credits, or offsets of state and local income taxes (see page 22) . .	10
11	Alimony received	11
12	Business income or (loss). Attach Schedule C or C-EZ	12
13	Capital gain or (loss). Attach Schedule D if required. If not required, check here ▶ ☐	13
14	Other gains or (losses). Attach Form 4797	14
15a	Total IRA distributions . 15a _____ b Taxable amount (see page 23)	15b
16a	Total pensions and annuities 16a _____ b Taxable amount (see page 23)	16b
17	Rental real estate, royalties, partnerships, S corporations, trusts, etc. Attach Schedule E	17
18	Farm income or (loss). Attach Schedule F	18
19	Unemployment compensation	19
20a	Social security benefits . 20a _____ b Taxable amount (see page 25)	20b
21	Other income. List type and amount (see page 27) _____	21
22	Add the amounts in the far right column for lines 7 through 21. This is your **total income** ▶	22

Adjusted Gross Income

23	IRA deduction (see page 27)	23
24	Student loan interest deduction (see page 28)	24
25	Archer MSA deduction. Attach Form 8853	25
26	Moving expenses. Attach Form 3903	26
27	One-half of self-employment tax. Attach Schedule SE .	27
28	Self-employed health insurance deduction (see page 30)	28
29	Self-employed SEP, SIMPLE, and qualified plans . .	29
30	Penalty on early withdrawal of savings	30
31a	Alimony paid **b** Recipient's SSN ▶ _____	31a
32	Add lines 23 through 31a	32
33	Subtract line 32 from line 22. This is your **adjusted gross income** . . . . . ▶	33

For Disclosure, Privacy Act, and Paperwork Reduction Act Notice, see page 72.   Cat. No. 11320B   Form **1040** (2001)

This diagram provides an overview of the expenses and of the sources of income for the U.S. government.

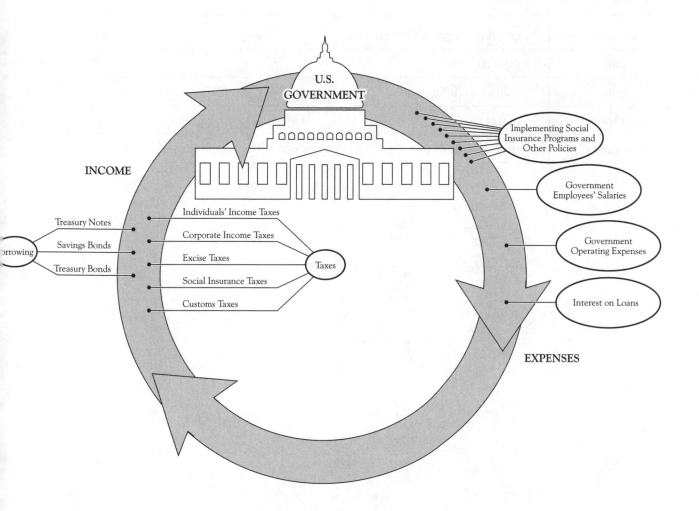

INCOME

Treasury Notes

Savings Bonds

Treasury Bonds

Borrowing

Individuals' Income Taxes

Corporate Income Taxes

Excise Taxes

Social Insurance Taxes

Customs Taxes

Taxes

U.S. GOVERNMENT

Implementing Social Insurance Programs and Other Policies

Government Employees' Salaries

Government Operating Expenses

Interest on Loans

EXPENSES

Word Power

The words on the following chart are underscored in the section called "What Your Child Needs to Know." Explain their meanings to your child as needed when they come up in reading or discussion. Keep the list handy for you and your child to use.

Word	Definition
allocated	given for a particular purpose
compiles	puts together
compute	calculate, figure out
corresponds	matches
revenue	the amount of money a government collects for public use

What Your Child Needs to Know

You may choose to use the following text in several different ways, depending on your child's strengths and preferences. You might read the passage aloud; you might read it to yourself and then paraphrase it for your child; or you might ask your child to read the material along with you or on his or her own.

INTRODUCTION TO TAXING AND SPENDING

As discussed in Chapter 7, domestic and foreign policies are plans for ensuring that the United States will provide the best possible quality of life for its citizens. But after policy is written and approved, it must be put into action. Putting policy into action takes a great deal of money. How does the U.S. government raise the money to pay for textbooks, public health care, tunnels and bridges, and public housing projects? How does it get the money to support democratic nations abroad and pay for our military defense program? The federal government gets its money primarily by collecting taxes and by borrowing money.

THE GOVERNMENT TAKES IN MONEY

The framers of the Constitution believed that government should be responsible for providing its citizens with many important functions and services. They realized also that the government would need money to provide these things. Consequently, the framers spelled out in the Constitution how the government should "have power to lay and collect taxes, duties, imposts, and excises, and to pay the debts and provide for the common defense and general welfare of the United States. . . ."

Taxes

Most of the U.S. government's income comes from tax money paid by citizens. The federal govern-

ment receives tax money from both individuals and companies. Various agencies in the executive branch collect several different kinds of taxes.

For example, nearly all adult American citizens pay **income taxes** to their state governments and to the federal government. (Most citizens pay taxes to their local government as well.) The federal government collects about 45 percent of its tax revenue—between $400 billion and $500 billion—from individuals' income taxes. Not everyone pays the same amount of tax money to the government, however. People pay taxes according to their income, so that wealthy people pay higher taxes than people who make less money.

Tax payments are due to the government each year on April 15. Instead of telling American citizens how much money they owe in taxes, the U.S. government leaves the responsibility of figuring out the correct amount to citizens themselves. To pay their taxes, Americans compute how much money they owe using a form called a **tax return.** Then they send checks to the **Internal Revenue Service (IRS).** This federal government agency, a part of the Department of the Treasury, is in charge of collecting and processing taxes from citizens. Employees of the IRS check to make sure that tax returns have been filled out correctly, and they make note of any returns that they believe should be **audited,** or checked more carefully for errors. In some cases, by auditing tax returns, the IRS discovers that some individuals are trying to deceive the government about how much money they owe. Intentionally cheating the government on a tax return is a serious crime called **tax fraud.**

Companies must pay **corporate income taxes** to the U.S. government. Of course, some companies have enormous amounts of money, and many of these businesses must send large sums in tax money to the IRS. Corporate income taxes account for about 10 percent of the nation's total tax revenue. Some types of organizations, such as schools and churches, are not required to pay any income tax at all.

The government collects **social insurance taxes** to pay for many of the social services outlined in Chapter 7, such as social security, unemployment insurance, and the Medicare and Medicaid programs. These taxes account for about 36 percent of federal tax revenue—hundreds of billions of dollars each year.

Excise taxes are money added to the prices of things such as automobiles, gasoline, airline tickets, cigarettes, liquor, and long-distance telephone service. When people buy such items or services, part of the money they pay goes to the federal government. Excise taxes make up only about 4 percent of the nation's tax revenue—approximately $40 billion each year. Because people do not pay excise taxes on food or other things that are strictly necessary, these taxes are sometimes referred to as **luxury taxes.**

Another type of tax, **customs duties,** is added to the prices of goods that are imported from other countries to be sold in the United States. The U.S. Congress has power to make decisions about which imported products shall be taxed and at what rate. The government uses customs duties in two ways. First, this tax is simply a source of money for the government. Congress also uses customs duties to discourage the sale of certain imported items by making them more expensive than similar products made in the United States by American workers. Discouraging the sale of imported goods protects American business by promoting the sale of goods produced in this country. Customs duties bring in a little less than $20 billion each year.

Borrowing

Taxes almost never bring in enough money to pay for all of the federal government's expenses. Therefore, the government must collect more money. To do this, it "borrows" money from the American people by selling them Treasury notes and Treasury bonds, savings bonds, and other federal certificates and notes. These are actually pieces of paper that say that a person has lent money to the government. The government has use of that money until years later, when the citizen cashes in the bond. Then his or her money will be returned with **interest,** or extra money paid by the government to the person for the use of his or her money. The interest is a certain percentage of the original cost of the note or bond. People who lend money to the government by buying a note or bond make a profit because they get back more money than they paid. Next to individual income taxes and social insurance taxes, borrowing is the

next largest source of income for the federal government. In recent years, the government has borrowed about $275 billion a year.

The U.S. government has been borrowing in this way for several decades because it has been unable to raise enough money through taxation to cover its expenses. This borrowing has taken its toll on the government's pocketbook because of the interest the government must pay. Consequently, the government has run up an enormous **national debt,** or total amount of money it owes. In the 1980s, some economic experts and government leaders began speaking out about the importance of reducing (and eventually paying off) the national debt. It is a difficult goal that continues to challenge the U.S. government to this day.

SPENDING

The federal government has many expenses, including the salaries it pays to its more than 3 million employees. In addition, the government spends money for all of the supplies and services it uses every day. Then, of course, it spends vast sums of money to support existing government programs and to put government policies into effect. Recently, the United States has spent more than $1 trillion a year. Following is a summary of the three main ways that this money goes back to the people.

1. Nearly half of this trillion dollars is spent on payments that go directly to individuals in the form of social security checks, money for Medicaid and Medicare claims, unemployment benefits—money paid to help support people who are out of work—and so forth. Such payments account for more money than the government spends for any other program.
2. For nearly a century, the United States has held the position of the most powerful democratic nation in the world. To maintain this position, the federal government has spent many hundreds of billions of dollars each year on **national defense**—in other words, on weapons, military equipment and facilities, and soldiers and other military personnel. About a quarter of the government's spending each year goes to national security and defense.
3. The third use of federal money is support of state and local governments around the na-

tion. These governments distribute some of this money to social service agencies and use the rest to pay for things such as roads and highways, police protection, and construction projects.

THE FEDERAL BUDGET

Like individuals and families around the nation, the federal government uses a budget, or plan, to predict how much money it will take in and how much it will spend each year. The government's budget is extremely complicated, of course. In fact, because the task of preparing a budget for the U.S. government takes so long (about a year and a half), thousands of federal employees in the executive and legislative branches do nothing but work on budgets. Unlike most personal or family budgets, the federal budget does not begin on January 1 and end on December 31 of each year. Instead, the federal budget <u>corresponds</u> to a **fiscal,** or financial, year that begins each October 1 and ends each September 30.

The Budget Process

The president is responsible for proposing a federal budget. The president uses this responsibility as an opportunity to announce to other government leaders and to the American people as a whole what the White House believes are the country's most pressing issues and concerns. By shaping the budget in certain ways, the president can send a dramatic political message about the way the executive branch sees our nation and the world. Of course, the "nuts and bolts" of the budget are gathered and assembled not by the president, but by the thousands of people in various departments and agencies of the executive branch.

The long budget-planning process begins when each department or agency in the executive branch makes a list of its wants and needs for the upcoming budget. This happens in the spring, a year and a half before the proposed budget would begin. Each agency notes how much money it wishes to spend on every new or continuing program. Agencies send these plans to the Office of Management and Budget (OMB).

The director of the OMB <u>compiles</u> all the plans and takes them to the president so that both of

them may get an idea of how the new budget might look. Along with economic and policy advisers, the president and the OMB director study the budget to determine whether the government will be able to collect enough tax money to pay for it. In other words, they ask if the government will be able to achieve a **balanced budget**—a budget that does not call for spending more money than is available. If not, how much would the government need to add to the national debt by borrowing additional funds?

Then the president and the advisers decide whether they want to make changes regarding which government departments get how much money. Finally the president decides how much money will be <u>allocated</u> to each department and agency. The president sends recommendations to the various departments and agencies.

Around the end of the summer, each agency works hard to prepare its final budget requests according to the president's recommendations. By fall, the OMB has in hand these revised requests from each agency. Once again, budget plans are submitted to the president for final adjustments and approval. The president usually takes a few months to make final changes to the budget before submitting it to Congress by the deadline of January 1.

The Role of Congress

Both the president and the U.S. Congress play important roles in creating the budget for the federal government, and these roles illustrate the value of checks and balances in American government. Though the president presents a complete budget to Congress, that document has no power until Congress approves it. The Constitution grants Congress the right to change the president's budget however it wishes. And the fact is that Congress never accepts the president's budget proposal without plenty of revision. Even when the president's party is the majority party in Congress, there is almost always conflict over the budget between the two government branches. It seems that various government leaders will always have different ideas about how—and how much—money should be gotten and spent.

A budget moves through the Congress in three basic steps.

1. Two standing committees (see Chapter 4), the **Senate Budget Committee** and the **House Budget Committee,** take three months to analyze the president's budget. By April 15, these committees prepare revisions of that proposal.
2. Between April 15 and June 15, a variety of Congressional committees take a hard look at the revisions. Committee members analyze the proposed plans for spending, and at the same time they consider the government's plan for taxing and borrowing. Between June 15 and 30, both houses of Congress must approve any changes and adjustments made to the budget.
3. The final step of the process involves the Office of Management and Budget. If the president and Congress have together hammered out a proposed budget that would add to the nation's national debt, the OMB trims the budget further to avoid increasing the debt.

 Implications

> To answer the question, "Why does all this matter?" or "What does it mean?," share the following insights with your child.

- **Through tax payments, American citizens themselves pay for the many public services and programs legislated by elected officials in Washington, D.C.** It surprises some people to learn that the government has no money other than that which it collects (primarily from citizens and corporations) in the form of taxes. It is, perhaps, too common for Americans to conceive of government as a distant and powerful entity that bears little direct relation to their lives. A healthier—and more accurate—view is that the government is the people: not only do citizens elect individuals to work for them in government, but also citizens pay to operate the government and to put into effect the policies elected leaders devise.
- **Just as being in debt takes away economic power from individuals, the U.S. government's national debt weakens the nation economically.** Starting in the 1980s, government leaders knowingly piled up a huge national debt. Many economists have spoken about the crucial importance of eliminating that debt. Despite the fact that having the opportunity to profit from interest paid on government bonds and notes seems to benefit American citizens, in the long run, U.S. citizens are hurt by the debt those interest payments incur.

 Fact Checker

> To check that your child knows or can find the basic facts in this chapter, here is an activity based on information discussed.

Match the terms in the column on the left with their definitions or descriptions in the column on the right.

1. individual income taxes
2. Internal Revenue Service
3. social insurance taxes
4. excise taxes
5. customs duties
6. national debt
7. Federal Reserve Bank
8. national budget

a. government agency in charge of collecting taxes
b. taxes on luxuries
c. government's plan for taxing and spending
d. federal government's banking agency
e. most of the government's income
f. taxes to pay for social security
g. taxes on imported goods
h. the money owed by the government

Answers appear in the back, preceding the index.

The Big Questions

The following questions encourage your child to think critically rather than simply recall facts. If necessary, review the specific information from the preceding pages that will help your child make the appropriate inferences to come up with reasonable answers.

1. Often, candidates for political office promise voters that they will lower taxes. Can you think of arguments both for and against lowering taxes?
2. Most individual taxpayers pay taxes to support government programs that will never benefit them directly. For example, even if a person will never be unemployed, his or her taxes will help provide money for people who are out of work. Do you think this is fair? Why or why not?

Suggested Answers

1. *An argument for lowering taxes is that it would allow citizens to keep more of the money they make, which means they would have more money to spend. An argument against lowering taxes is that if the government has less money, it has less funding for important social programs.*
2. *Children should understand that government programs improve the quality of life for our society as a whole—not every program benefits each individual. In the long run, living in a society in which as many people as possible have access to the necessities of life benefits everyone.*

Skills Practice

The following activities give your child practice in applying the skills basic to social studies. For some of the activities, your child may need to review the information in the preceding pages.

A. *WRITING A SUMMARY*

Students are often asked to summarize in social studies classes and in language arts classes.

Go over in your mind what you have learned about the national debt or reread the section of this chapter that contains an explanation of the national debt. Then write a short paragraph summarizing what you know about this subject.

Suggested Answer

Because the U.S. government does not raise all the money it needs for its programs from income taxes, it needs to borrow money. The main way the government does this is to sell people bonds and Treasury notes.

Years later, when people cash in their bonds and notes, the government pays them back their money with interest. The money that the government owes these people accounts for most of the national debt. The national debt has become very large, and the government is trying to pay it off.

Evaluating Your Child's Skills: In order to complete this activity successfully, your child needs to have a sound understanding of the required information and the ability to focus on the most important ideas. If necessary, go over the section of the chapter that explains the national debt. With your child, list the points it makes. The list can serve as a basis for a summary. (In order to answer successfully, your child should make most of the points in the suggested answer, but not necessarily all of them. The important thing is for him or her to show understanding of the facts presented in the chapter.)

B. MAKING AND INTERPRETING A PIE CHART

Being able to show information in a visual way is an important skill that will help your child enhance his or her social studies reports. Being able to interpret visual information is an important skill in many subjects.

A pie chart starts with a circle. The circle represents the whole amount of something. In this case, the circle will represent all the money the government took in during the year 1995. By dividing the circle, you can show how much of this money came from different sources.

Directions: Draw a circle. Use a ruler to divide the circle into eighths using light pencil marks. Make darker lines to section off three eighths. Label this section "Individual Income Tax." With darker lines, section off another three eighths. Label this section "Social Insurance Tax." Make a dark line to separate the two remaining eighths. Label one "Corporate Income Tax" and the other "Other Taxes." (The other taxes include excise taxes and customs duties.) Finally, erase the light pencil lines that are showing. Color each section of the pie chart a different color.

Questions

To interpret, or translate, your chart into actual information, answer the following questions.

1. In 1995, what were the two biggest sources of income for the government?
2. What were the two smallest?
3. About what fraction of its total income would the government have lost in 1995 if people had not paid income tax?

4. About what fraction of its total income would the government have lost if corporations had not paid taxes?

Answers

Check to see that your child's chart matches the directions given.

1. *Individual Income Tax and Social Insurance Tax*
2. *Corporate Income Tax and Other Taxes*
3. *About three-eighths*
4. *About one-eighth*

Evaluating Your Child's Skills: In order to complete this activity successfully, your child must be able to follow written directions and translate visual information into verbal information. If necessary, review the simple math needed to answer the interpretation questions.

Top of the Class

Children interested in delving more deeply into the topics covered in this chapter can choose one or more of the following activities. They may do the activities for their own satisfaction or report in class on what they have done to show that they have been seriously considering how and why the government taxes and spends.

RESEARCH

Suggest to your child that he or she do research in the children's section of the library to find out the meanings and implications of the terms *recession* and *inflation*.

In the children's room of your local library or in your school library, do research that will help you learn the meanings of the terms *recession* and *inflation*. You could look for a book that explains economics in a simple way, or you could look up the terms in a children's encyclopedia. Read about the problems related to both recession and inflation and how the government tries to control both. You may want to present your findings in a short written or oral report.

BOOKS TO READ AND RECOMMEND IN CLASS

Suggest that your child read the following nonfiction books and respond to them by giving an oral or written critique in class.

Sendak, Cass R. *The National Debt* (*Inside Government* series). Twenty-First Century, 1996.

Worth, Richard. *Poverty* (*Overview* series). Lucent, 1997.

CHAPTER 9
State Government

This chart provides an overview of the organization of the three branches of state government.

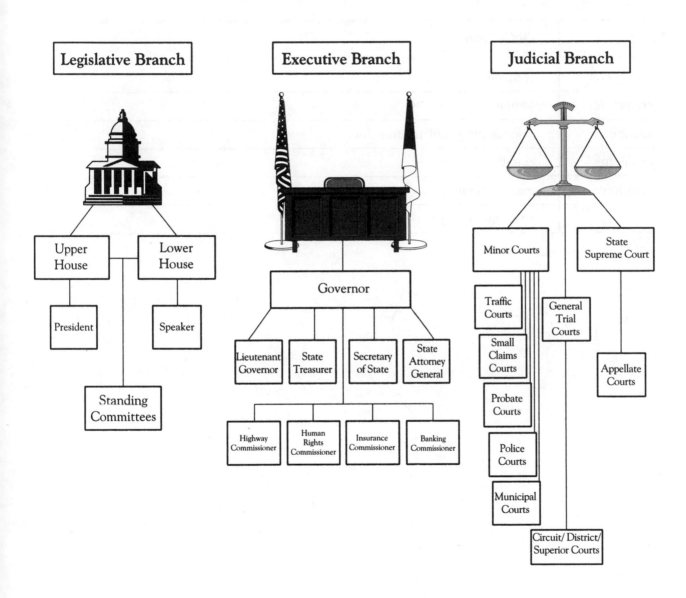

Legislative Branch

Upper House — President

Lower House — Speaker

Standing Committees

Executive Branch

Governor

Lieutenant Governor | State Treasurer | Secretary of State | State Attorney General

Highway Commissioner | Human Rights Commissioner | Insurance Commissioner | Banking Commissioner

Judicial Branch

Minor Courts

Traffic Courts

Small Claims Courts

Probate Courts

Police Courts

Municipal Courts

Circuit/ District/ Superior Courts

General Trial Courts

State Supreme Court

Appellate Courts

Word Power

The words on the following chart chart below are underscored in the section called "What Your Child Needs to Know." Explain their meanings to your child as needed when they come up in reading or discussion. Keep the list handy for you and your child to use.

Word	*Definition*
administered	controlled
comparable	similar
daunting	discouraging, difficult to achieve
equivalent	equal
regulation	management
revive	give new strength to something

What Your Child Needs to Know

You may choose to use the following text in several different ways, depending on your child's strengths and preferences. You might read the passage aloud; you might read it to yourself and then paraphrase it for your child; or you might ask your child to read the material along with you or on his or her own.

INTRODUCTION TO STATE GOVERNMENT

Throughout our nation's history, governmental leaders and ordinary citizens have debated this question: how should power be divided between the federal government and state governments? History shows that it is an important question. After all, the nation got off to a rocky start because of the imbalance of power between the federal governments and the governments of the individual states (see Chapter 1).

Then, at the Constitutional Convention in 1787, the nation's political leaders agreed that a proper balance between the state governments and the federal government was essential and that the U.S. Constitution should specify how power should be divided or shared between the states and the federal government. This chapter explains the organization and the functions of state governments.

State Constitutions

As the U.S. government is established and defined by the U.S. Constitution, each of the nation's state governments is established and defined by a **state constitution.** The fifty state constitutions vary in age, length, and level of detail. Some states have used the same constitution for dozens of generations. Since becoming a state in 1820, for example, Maine has relied on only one constitution. Other states have rewritten their constitutions. Georgia, for instance, adopted its present constitution quite recently, in 1982. Over the years, all fifty state constitutions have been lengthened and changed through amendments. Regardless of its age or its length, though, any state constitution stands as the supreme law of its state. In terms of legal authority, only the U.S. Constitution stands above it.

Each state constitution serves several important purposes.

- *It establishes the organization or structure of the state government.*
- *It outlines the powers or functions of each part of the state government.*
- *It lays the foundation for* **local governments** *by establishing political divisions such as counties, boroughs, parishes, townships, and municipalities.*

THE ORGANIZATION AND FUNCTIONS OF STATE GOVERNMENTS

All states mirror the federal government in being divided into executive, legislative, and judicial branches. Each state constitution outlines this structure in some detail. Each branch is made up of many specific departments and agencies that have particular powers and responsibilities. As Washington, D.C., is the capital of our entire country, each state has a capital city with a capitol building that houses the state legislature and a house known as the *governor's mansion,* which is the residence of the state's current governor.

The Executive Branch

The executive branch of state government is roughly <u>equivalent</u> to the executive branch of the federal government, and the office of **governor** is basically similar to the presidency. Because the responsibilities and functions of the two offices are <u>comparable</u>, serving as governor is considered good training for future presidents. In fact, several presidents, including George W. Bush, Bill Clinton, Ronald Reagan, and Franklin D. Roosevelt, served as governors before they were elected to the presidency.

Governors have great power and influence in state government. Perhaps a governor's most important function is overseeing its budget. As chief executive, the governor usually supervises all departments and agencies of the executive branch as they work to carry out state laws. This can be a

State capitol building, Des Moines, Iowa

daunting task because some state governments contain a dizzying number of agencies and also because some state constitutions do not grant governors *complete* control over the executive branch. In these cases, a governor may compete with other elected officials in the executive branch to get legislation put into practice. Any of these other officials may have different ideas about running the state's affairs and solving its problems. Some may even represent a different political party from that of the governor.

In most states, the executive branch includes the following important officials.

- The **state attorney general** is the state's most powerful legal official. This person oversees all of the state's activities involving the law. Specifically, a state attorney general can serve as legal adviser to the governor as well as represent the state as its lawyer.
- The **secretary of state** is the chief clerk, or secretary, in charge of all official state documents and records.
- The **state treasurer** is the state's highest financial official. This person oversees the payment of bills the state owes. Often, the state treasurer is also in charge of collecting state income taxes.

- The **lieutenant governor** has a role similar to that of the nation's vice president. A lieutenant governor presides over the state senate and stands ready to replace the governor in the event of his or her serious illness or death.

Most governors work closely with the state legislative branch. In fact, one of a governor's most important functions is to propose new laws and programs to the legislature. Like the nation's president, a governor has the power to veto or to approve legislation passed by a state legislature. Moreover, governors may appoint people for certain posts within the state government or remove them from these positions. Some of these positions are **highway commissioner, human rights commissioner, insurance commissioner,** and **banking commissioner.**

Many governors use their status as leaders to bring business to their states. Often, they travel around the nation—even around the globe—to form relationships with individuals and companies elsewhere. Sometimes governors use their influence to get financial help from the federal government. For instance, if a state suffers a natural disaster, its governor might appeal to the president for economic aid during the cleanup process.

The qualifications for governor vary from state to state, but most require an individual to be over thirty years old and to have been a U.S. citizen and a resident of his or her state for a specified period of time. Most people who are elected governor have had considerable experience in both local and state government.

Election campaigns for the office of governor usually begin with a **party primary,** at which major parties nominate their candidates. Third-party candidates may run as well. Then citizens of the state vote in a general election for governor. In forty-five states, the candidate who receives a **plurality,** or more votes than any other candidate, wins the election. However, in Arizona, Louisiana, Mississippi, Georgia, and Vermont, a candidate must win a **majority,** or more than half, of the votes. In nearly all states, governors serve four-year terms.

The Legislative Branch

Every one of the nation's fifty states has its own legislature. Just like the U.S. Congress, the legislative bodies of forty-nine states are bicameral, or divided into two houses. (The exception is Nebraska's **unicameral,** or one-chambered, legislative body.) As in the legislative branch of the federal government, the upper house is called the *senate.* The lower house is usually called the *house of representatives,* though in some states it is named the *general assembly,* the *legislative assembly,* or the *general court.* On average, state senates are composed of about forty members. Minnesota's senate is the largest, with sixty-seven members, whereas Alaska's is the smallest, with twenty. On the other hand, the size of the states' lower houses vary widely and are not necessarily related to the sizes of the states. For example, the nation's largest state, Alaska, has forty members in its house of representatives, whereas the lower house of one of the nation's smallest states, New Hampshire, has four hundred members.

Most state constitutions set term limits for state legislators. Usually state senators serve for four years and state representatives serve for two years. To qualify for the state legislature, a person must have a legal residence in a particular voting district in a state and must meet an age requirement (usu-ally twenty-five years or older for the senate and twenty-one years for the house). In dramatic contrast to federal legislators, state senators and representatives work only part-time. This is because state legislatures are not in session all the time. For example, the Texas legislature meets once every *other* year. However, the majority of state legislatures do meet at least once, if not twice, annually. Since most elected positions in state government are not highly paid, many state politicians have careers in fields outside of politics.

As a rule, state legislatures are structured and administered much as the U.S. Congress is. For example, both houses of the state legislature have leaders to help them function effectively. More than half of the state senates are led by lieutenant governors. This position is much like the president of the U.S. Senate (a position filled by the vice president of the United States) in the sense that it carries little real power except the right to break voting ties. In the senates of twenty-three states, however, leadership falls to a much more powerful **senate president.**

Each state's house of representatives is led by a speaker of the house whose duties are almost identical to those of the federal House Speaker. The house speaker runs house sessions, controls who can speak during those sessions and when issues will be put to a vote, and decides who will serve on legislative committees. In most state legislatures, the house speaker has an important additional power: appointing the chairpersons of various legislative committees.

Just as in the U.S. Congress, committees do much of the day-to-day work of state legislatures. Most states have about thirty standing committees to handle issues such as transportation, education, police protection, and welfare. Most state legislators serve on several standing committees. All work to create and pass laws to benefit society in their states.

The Judicial Branch

State laws govern much of what we do in our daily lives. When state laws are broken, cases are heard in state courtrooms by state judges. In fact, in the United States, far more cases are tried in state courts than in federal courts. In fact, whereas federal judges hear about 250,000 cases during the course of an average year, state judges hear a total of approximately 25 million cases each year. Typical violations of state law range from robbery and assault to the failure to use a turn signal when changing lanes in a car or truck.

State court systems across the nation handle cases involving both civil law and criminal law. As explained in Chapter 5, civil law usually involves disputes between two persons or private groups. Occasionally, civil cases involve conflicts between an individual (or a private organization) and the state government. Criminal law involves cases in which the state government prosecutes an individual for breaking a state law. Criminal cases focus on two levels of crime. On one hand, **misdemeanors** are minor crimes that require relatively minor punishments. These crimes include most traffic violations, as well as social offenses such as littering or creating a public disturbance. In contrast, **felonies** are serious and major crimes that call for jail sentences or, in some states, the death penalty. Examples of felonies include arson, rape, burglary, and murder.

Though states use a variety of names for different types of state courts, these courts generally fall into three categories. There are so many kinds of courts within each category that just a few examples are given here.

- **Minor courts** handle misdemeanor cases that come up in the course of daily life. Some minor courts handle specific types of cases. For instance, **traffic courts** deal with parking violations and other offenses involving motor vehicles. **Small claims courts** handle civil disputes over small amounts of money.
- **General trial courts** deal only with felonies. These courts might be called **circuit courts,** district courts, or some other name, depending on the state.
- Appellate, or appeals, courts hear cases that have been tried in general trial courts and are being appealed (see Chapter 5). The highest appeals court on the state level is usually called the **state supreme court.** This court also stands as the highest authority on interpreting the state constitution and all state laws.

Different states select state judges in different ways. In many states, judges are elected by voters. In other states, judges are elected by the state legislature. In still others, judges are appointed by the governor. Finally, in some states, judges are selected by a method called the **Missouri Plan,** which allows governors to appoint most state judges. Then it gives final approval for these appointments to citizens in a popular election.

ADDITIONAL FUNCTIONS OF STATE GOVERNMENTS

The most powerful governmental figures in our nation are part of the federal government in Washington, D.C. It may be this simple fact that causes many people to perceive state government as less important or less powerful than the federal government. However, it is state governments that make and pass the policies and laws that dominate our everyday lives. Of course, state governments must raise tax money from citizens and collect money from the federal government in order to implement these laws and policies. State governments are responsible for funding and managing everything from public schools and hospitals to police departments and public assistance programs. A few of the most important functions and powers of state government are described in the following paragraphs.

Law Enforcement

The executive and legislative branches of state government create, pass, and implement the state laws that shape our lives. Of course, those laws must be enforced. While much of the police work across our nation is performed by local police departments, every state maintains a state police force as well. These state police departments focus much of their attention on traffic safety on state and federal highways. Occasionally they work together with local police forces to investigate other crimes that threaten the property or well-being of citizens.

State governments administer state prisons, county prisons, and local jails. Individuals who are given jail sentences for breaking state laws serve their punishments in state prisons.

Business, Labor, and the Workplace

One of the most important ways in which state governments affect the lives of citizens is in the world of business and work. For example, governors and other state leaders try continually to persuade businesses to relocate in their states. State government leaders do this because more business usually means a healthier economy, more jobs, and a higher standard of living for the state's residents. Yet state governments cannot be entirely pro-business. Without regulation by government, some companies might treat workers or the local environment in ways that are unfair or harmful. Consequently, state government must regulate the activities of businesses, the conditions of workplaces, the treatment of laborers, and any related environmental issues.

Some types of businesses have been singled out for special attention by regulatory groups within state government.

- States oversee insurance companies in order to make sure that they do not charge rates that are unfair to consumers.
- State regulation of banks prevents them from profiting unfairly by making customers pay unreasonably high interest rates on loans.
- States regulate the rates public utilities charge for necessary products such as water, electricity, fuel, public transportation, and telephone service.
- States protect consumers from other unfair or dangerous business practices. These might include false advertising; improper licensing of professionals such as physicians, engineers, or accountants; or dishonesty in the sale of goods or services.

The Environment

During the last several decades, leaders of state government have needed to take steps to revive and protect the environment in their states. This has been necessary because people have damaged or threatened the environment so seriously and in so many different ways. Ironically, because the worst offenders in this respect are often businesses and industries, a state may very well endanger its own environment by encouraging the very business activity that helps the state to enjoy economic success.

Now states oversee the preservation of their natural resources, including land, waterways, and animal life. State laws and policies limit the negative effects that companies can have on the environment. Individuals or corporations that wish to construct new facilities are required by many states to provide proof that such building projects will not harm the local ecology.

Social Services

The majority of spending by state governments goes to social service programs. The three most important recipients of state money are public education, public health, and public assistance. In fact, states spend nearly two-thirds of all available funds in these three areas.

- States take responsibility for providing public health facilities and public health care for their citizens. Consequently, state money is needed to pay for salaries of physicians, nurses, laboratory workers, and other workers, as well as equipment and maintenance of hospitals and clinics. The federal government provides about half of the funds needed for these services, and state governments raise the other half.
- In partnership with the federal government, state government administers public assistance programs for needy citizens. This takes the form of federal social insurance programs—Medicare, social security, and unemployment insurance—as well as federal public assistance programs, such as Aid to Families with Dependent Children. In addition, most states have developed assistance programs to serve state residents who don't qualify for programs designed by the federal government.
- A century ago, the federal government provided the majority of the money needed for **public education.** Now state governments outspend Washington by a great deal. Consequently, states have more power and influence over how public schools are run. A state establishes local school districts, sets educational guidelines ranging from the number of school days each year to the types of subjects public schools may teach, and provides funds for educational materials, salaries, and so on. State spending on education does not stop with high school. In fact, states spend more on public

colleges and universities than they do on any other level of education.

Implications

To answer the question, "Why does all this matter?" or "What does it mean?," share the following insights with your child.

• **The balance of power between the federal government and state governments gives the nation unity as well as diversity.** Federal law unites our nation's fifty states in certain fundamental ways. For example, Americans in any state can vote for president after they reach the age of eighteen. Yet the nation is made up of fifty states with unique sets of state laws and policies. For example, young people in Louisiana can become licensed drivers of automobiles as early as age fourteen, whereas citizens of Colorado must wait until age twenty-one to obtain a regular driver's license. In many states, children must attend school beginning at age five; yet in Pennsylvania and in the state of Washington, children are not legally required to attend school until age eight.

• **Though state senators, state representatives, and state judges are less well known than their federal counterparts, informed voting for state politicians and judicial officials is vital to a healthy democracy.** Since so many aspects of Americans' daily lives are affected directly by state laws, citizens should recognize that state elections are just as important as federal elections. Voters should carefully choose the elected officials who will create and promote policies and laws and put them into practice.

Fact Checker

To check that your child knows or can find the basic facts in this chapter, here is an activity based on information discussed.

Use the words in the word bank to fill in the blanks in the following sentences.

1. The chief executive of a state is the state's _____.

2. In state government, the equivalent of the vice president is the _____ governor.

3. Whereas the president lives in the White House, the governor of a state lives in the governor's _____.

4. Public schools in a state are regulated by the _____ government.

5. In some states, _____ are appointed by the governor, while in others they are elected.

6. Like the federal government, most states have _____ legislatures.

7. Like the president, a governor is elected for a _____-year term of office.

Word Bank

lieutenant	state	bicameral
four	judges	mansion	governor

Answers appear in the back, preceding the index.

The Big Questions

The following questions encourage your child to think critically rather than simply recall facts. If necessary, review the specific information from the preceding pages that will help your child make the appropriate inferences to come up with reasonable answers.

Why does each state need its own government, complete with three branches, a constitution,

and the right to collect taxes from citizens? Why isn't it enough to have a federal government, with perhaps small local governments to run towns and cities?

Suggested Answers

The United States is too big to be governed by one central government. Also, the states are so different from one another that they have different needs and their citizens have different ways of life. Each state needs a government that will focus on the needs of its own citizens.

Skills Practice

The following activities give your child practice in applying the skills basic to social studies. For some of the activities, your child may need to review the information in the preceding pages.

A. MAKING A VENN DIAGRAM

Being able to show information in a visual way is an important skill that will help your child enhance his or her social studies reports.

Draw a Venn diagram—two overlapping circles. Make sure the overlapping part of the diagram is large enough to write in. Label the left-hand circle "Federal" and the other "State." Label the overlapping area "Federal and State." In the left-hand circle, write two or three things that are true of the federal government but are *not* true of state governments. In the right-hand circle, write two or three things that are true of state governments but are *not* true of the federal government. In the overlapping area in the middle, write two or three things that are true of *both* the federal and state governments.

Suggested Answers

Federal: *Chief executive is the president; legislators work full-time; all judges appointed by the president.*

State: *Chief executive is the governor; legislators work part-time; some judges are elected.*

Both: *Has a constitution; government has three branches; collects taxes.*

***Evaluating Your Child's Skills:* In order to complete this activity successfully, your child must be able to follow written directions and translate verbal information into visual information. If your child needs help understanding how a Venn diagram works, make one showing differences and similarities between two members of your family or two rooms in your home.**

B. WRITING A PARAGRAPH OF COMPARISON

> Practice in writing comparison paragraphs will help your child with his or her social studies, language arts, and science assignments.

Using what you have learned from this chapter, write a paragraph comparing the federal government with state governments. That is, show how the two types of governments are alike. Don't make your paragraph too long. Choose only the points that you think are most important to understanding how the two kinds of government are similar.

Suggested Answer

State governments are structured in a way that is very similar to the federal government. Both state governments and the federal government have three branches: executive, legislative, and judicial. In both types of government, the executive branch has a chief executive. Almost all the state legislatures, like the federal legislature, have a senate and a house of representatives. Both judicial branches have a supreme court and a system of lower courts. In addition, each state government, like the federal government, has a constitution. A state government is, in many ways, like a mini federal government.

> ***Evaluating Your Child's Skills:*** In order to complete this activity successfully, your child needs to see clearly how state governments mirror the federal government. In addition, he or she needs to know how to structure a paragraph, stating the main idea in a topic sentence, supporting the main idea with details, and ending with a concluding, or summarizing, sentence. If necessary, suggest details your child needs to add or take out of his or her paragraph. Of course, your child does not need to end up with a paragraph exactly like the preceding one.

Top of the Class

> Children interested in delving more deeply into the topics covered in this chapter can choose one or more of the following activities. They may do the activities for their own satisfaction or report in class on what they have done to show that they have been seriously considering the structure and functioning of state governments.

RESEARCH: YOUR STATE GOVERNMENT

> Suggest to your child that he or she find out the names of your state's most important officials and, if possible, a little bit about them.

You probably know the name of your state's governor and can recognize him or her in a photograph. But do you know the other people who govern your state? Use a search engine on the Internet to find out who they are. Start your search by typing in the name of your state as a key word.

YOUR STATE CONSTITUTION

> Suggest that your child become familiar with your state's constitution.

In the library or on the Internet, you can find a copy of your state's constitution. You may not want to read the whole thing, but look it over. Then compare it with the U.S. Constitution. What similarities and differences do you notice?

BOOK TO READ AND RECOMMEND IN CLASS

Suggest that your child read the following nonfiction book and respond to it by giving an oral or written critique in class. From this book, children can find out a lot about their own states. In the library, encourage your child to look for a whole book that is just about your state.

Bock, Judy, and Rachel Kranz. *Encyclopedia of the United States.* Scholastic, 1997. Basic information, including general description, statistics, history, points of interest, and fascinating facts about each state in the United States. Illustrated with photos.

CHAPTER 10
Local Government

3 Types of Municipal Government

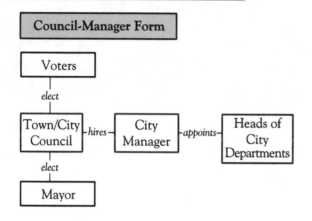

Council-Manager Form

Voters —elect→ Town/City Council —hires→ City Manager —appoints→ Heads of City Departments

Town/City Council —elect→ Mayor

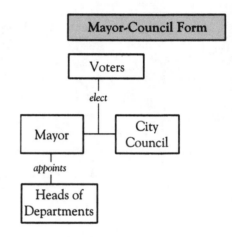

Mayor-Council Form

Voters —elect→ Mayor — City Council

Mayor —appoints→ Heads of Departments

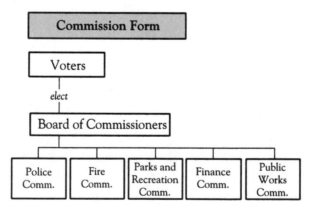

Commission Form

Voters —elect→ Board of Commissioners

Board of Commissioners:
- Police Comm.
- Fire Comm.
- Parks and Recreation Comm.
- Finance Comm.
- Public Works Comm.

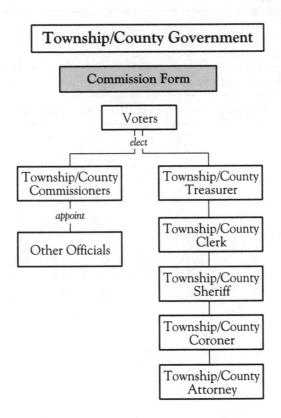

Township/County Government

Commission Form

Voters

elect

Township/County Commissioners

Township/County Treasurer

appoint

Other Officials

Township/County Clerk

Township/County Sheriff

Township/County Coroner

Township/County Attorney

Word Power

Word	Definition
administrators	supervisors; people who run an organization
complement	make a thing whole and perfect
eliminate	get rid of
extension	addition to, branch
prohibits	forbids, does not allow
subdivision	a part of something that is a part of an even larger entity

What Your Child Needs to Know

You may choose to use the following text in several different ways, depending on your child's strengths and preferences. You might read the passage aloud; you might read it to yourself and then paraphrase it for your child; or you might ask your child to read the material along with you or on his or her own.

INTRODUCTION TO LOCAL GOVERNMENT

Unlike state governments, local governments have no real legal independence or authority of their own. They are established and supervised by state governments, and their responsibilities and powers are determined by state governments. A state government can even decide to <u>eliminate</u> a local government. In other words, local government is an <u>extension</u> of state government. However, in large part, states give local governments freedom and power to manage themselves. Some states even grant larger cities **home rule**—the power to govern themselves independently of the state legislature.

SERVICES PROVIDED BY LOCAL GOVERNMENT

Most local governments provide, control, or supervise many programs and services. The most important of these are discussed as follows.

- Though federal and state governments maintain departments of education and develop policy concerning public education, local government almost always manages public schools and shapes public education within any given locality. In other words, local government officials control or oversee activities such as hiring teachers and <u>administrators</u>, enrolling and transporting students, maintaining school buildings and property, buying textbooks and other supplies, as well as making decisions on what subjects students should study and how they should be taught.

- Local government takes large responsibility for protecting citizens' lives and property. Usually, local governments spend nearly as much money on providing police and fire protection each year as they do on public education.

- Local governments play a crucial role in the way communities grow and change. Local **zoning laws,** for example, specify how certain types of land, buildings, or areas (zones) can be used. A city might pass a zoning law that <u>prohibits</u> factories in certain areas. Such a law would protect a residential neighborhood by keeping it quiet and attractive. Or it might pass a zoning law that does not allow a person to build a house on a piece of land that is less than a certain size. Such a law would ensure that a certain amount of open space would remain in the neighborhood.

- Local governments manage residents' water supplies and sanitation services. The state government leaves it to local officials to determine the best ways to give residents clean, safe water and the best systems to remove and process various types of garbage and waste.

- Many local governments handle a variety of programs involving transportation. Every local government must create and maintain streets, roads, and highways. In addition, many provide and maintain mass transit systems, such as bus, train, and subway service.

- Many local governments provide a range of free goods and **social services** to poor, handicapped, or unemployed citizens. These goods and services might include medical care, assistance in finding jobs, and even cash payments to be used for food or other necessities. Federal and state governments do contribute money toward such services, but some local governments must spend large amounts of money on them as well. Local governments also provide services such as transportation, meals, and social meeting places for senior citizens.

- Increasingly, local governments are spending money on **recreational** and **cultural activities** for residents. For example, a town or village might open a museum or offer programs for children or adults in theater or other performing arts, hiking or swimming, or arts and crafts.

Sources of Income for Local Government

Local government needs money to provide all of these services. The primary method of raising funds is by collecting **property taxes.** Residents pay taxes to the local government on all land, houses, and other buildings they own in that community. Local governments decide how much tax residents should pay by determining the amount of money the owners of property could expect to receive if the property were sold. Their property taxes are based on that amount.

Property taxes are by far the most important source of revenue for local governments. However, some communities collect additional income by charging a **sales tax** on many items that are sold in local stores. Not all states, however, permit local governments to charge sales tax. Also, local governments can collect **fines** for violations of traffic or sanitation laws. The money a person pays when he or she gets a parking ticket is an example of such a fine. A business could be fined for failing to have garbage removed from its property.

TYPES OF LOCAL GOVERNMENT

The term *local government* can refer to the governing body of four different types of **localities**—geographical and political divisions—within a state. They are the municipality, the county, the township, and the special district. All four do not exist in every state, however, and their powers differ from one state to another. A **county** is usually the largest subdivision of a state. It may contain a number of cities, towns, and villages. A **township,** in some states, is a large subdivision of a county. In some states, *township* is just another name for **town**—a small community with a population of five thousand or less. A **municipality** may be a town, city, or section of a city that has a charter granted to it by a state. A **charter** is a written document that spells out the municipality's powers, responsibilities, structure, and boundaries. A **special district** is an area established for the purpose of administering one particular public service such as education, transportation, or water supply. A school district is an example of a special district.

The governing bodies of the four types of localities have different structures. Often they overlap one another in certain ways. For example, an aver-age American lives in a municipality as well as a county and two or more special districts. Ideally, the various forms of local government try to make their functions and responsibilities complement one another.

County Government

Counties vary greatly in size, population, and number around the nation. For example, California's San Bernardino County has an area of more than 20,000 square miles, and the county's population is 1.7 million. By contrast, Los Angeles County is only 4,061 square miles in area, yet it boasts a population of almost 10 million citizens. The small state of Delaware is divided into only 3 counties, whereas Texas is carved into 254. In the state of Louisiana, counties are called *parishes;* Alaskans use the term *boroughs.* In all, there are 3,142 counties in the United States, each with its own government.

County governments help state governments administer policies and enforce laws. For example, county governments are responsible for maintaining roads and highways, county hospitals, county prisons, and regional airports. County governments control records and information involving elections, births and deaths, marriages, and the ownership of property. Sometimes county governments collect taxes, as well. Usually, county officials supervise voting places and voting practices during elections.

County governments can be structured in a variety of ways. Most are governed by an elected **county commission.** These commissions, which might be called the board of county commissioners, the board of freeholders, or the board of supervisors, handle matters such as budgets, taxes, and issues involving building and growth. They also have the power to appoint some officials. Other elected county officers, such as the country treasurer, county clerk, county sheriff, country coroner, and county attorney, may share power and responsibility with the county board.

Township Government

In twenty states, counties are divided into townships. These townships often provide services such as fire and police protection, water and sanitation services, and highway maintenance. The structure of township government is basically the same as that of county government.

In the states of New England, *township* is really another word for a village and its surrounding town. In some small New England towns, local government is still based around the **town meeting.** This gathering gives townspeople an opportunity to express their views and make decisions about the town's affairs. In this traditional New England town government system, elected officials called **selectmen** operate local government. In recent decades, town meetings have grown rarer, and selectmen (instead of the citizens themselves) are likely to make most decisions. Some towns have switched to a system in which an official called a **town manager** administrates local government.

Municipal Government

Discussions about municipalities can be confusing because the term *municipality* can refer to several different entities—cities, towns, and suburbs, for example, may all be municipalities. However, there are two basic characteristics of a municipality. First, a municipality must be an **urban** area, which most people think of as a city-like area, but which technically means a place with a population of at least twenty-five hundred people. Second, a municipality must have a charter from the state government, spelling out its legal rights, which include the right to issue contracts; to buy, own, and sell property; and to sue. A municipal charter also spells out the form the municipality's government will take. Virtually all municipal governments in the United States are of one of the three types described as follows.

- The **mayor-council** form of government is the most popular form of municipal government in the United States today. It is used by about half the nation's cities and by virtually all very large ones. This form of government favors the idea of separation of powers between the executive branch (an elected mayor) and the legislative branch (an elected council, usually composed of fewer than ten members). In this form of local government, the voters elect a mayor and members of a city council. The mayor appoints the heads of various city departments.
- The **council-manager** form of government also separates executive and legislative functions. More than 40 percent of American municipalities use the council-manager form of

local government. In this system, an elected council of five to nine members creates municipal policy. A town or city manager chosen by the council is the chief administrator, whose job it is to implement policy, oversee the budget, hire and fire municipal employees, and supervise the daily business of the municipality. The city manager appoints the heads of city departments. The council also elects a mayor, usually a council member. The mayor's powers, however, are quite limited.

- The **commission** form of government merges executive and legislative powers into a single governmental body of about half a dozen commissioners who are elected by voters. The commissioners head important municipal departments such as police, fire, parks and recreation, public works, and finance. Although one of the commissioners usually is named mayor, the only additional job that person has is to perform ceremonial functions such as greeting important visitors to the city. Less than 5 percent of American municipalities use the commission form of local government.

Special Districts

Most local governments create special districts to manage or administer certain public services. Often special districts cover a relatively large territory. For example, a single lake might provide the water supply for a dozen or more towns or cities in a state. To handle this situation, local government establishes a water district to provide this water to all residents of that area. This system avoids the complications that might occur if a dozen separate local governments tried to share a single water supply. Other special districts operate or supervise public schools; sewage and sanitation services; airports, tunnels and bridges; shipping ports; train stations and tracks; and roads and highways. In some cases, special districts use the term *commission* or *authority* in their names (as in *Massachusetts Transit Authority*).

INFLUENCING LOCAL GOVERNMENT

When people are unhappy about the actions—or sometimes the inaction—of their local government, they can sometimes take action to bring about changes in local government's working methods—or even in its policies.

On the most basic level, an individual can try to influence local government by writing a letter to a government official. However, especially in large communities, local officials receive so much correspondence that they may feel that they don't have enough time to respond to a question or suggestion from an individual person.

Consequently, many citizens find it more effective to contact local government officials as part of a community group formed for the purpose of taking political action. In some cases, an individual can join an already existing group; other times, he or she must form a brand-new group by finding and banding together with citizens who have similar views. Most local government officials are unwilling to ignore a complaint or suggestion received from a group of twenty, fifty, or one hundred citizens. Doing so might risk negative publicity and the loss of votes in upcoming elections.

Interest Groups

As special interest groups can affect federal and state government, they can also have important effects on local government. Here are examples of powerful interest groups at the local level.

- Because business leaders play such an important role in the life of a community—creating jobs, providing goods or services, lowering the property tax rates of residents—**business groups** often have little trouble getting the attention of local officials. For example, a single manufacturing plant might employ more than half of a town's residents. In such cases, the owners or managers of this company have a great deal of influence over government officials. Local officials know that such a company could move to another community if its requests or needs are not met. Other examples of important business groups are chambers of commerce and small business associations. The owners of local business get together and meet periodically for the purpose of communicating their interests to local government. For example, a group of store owners might try to influence their village government to provide money for a larger parking lot in order to draw more customers to their stores.
- In many local communities, residents from neighborhoods form **neighborhood groups** to protest or halt some development project. For example, a neighborhood group might be established to try to stop a private developer from building a twelve-story modern hotel in a neighborhood of small stores and homes.
- In large cities, labor unions sometimes exert influence over mayors and city councils. For example, why does the mayor of New York City listen to leaders of the labor union that represents police officers? One reason is that that labor union represents thousands of very influential potential voters.
- Finally, sometimes **political action groups** are organized around a particular issue or a specific part of the population. For example, in recent years, groups representing women, senior citizens, people with disabilities, and various ethnic or racial groups have grown extremely powerful in some American towns and cities.

Methods of Influencing Local Government Officials

The actual methods people use to try to affect local government vary widely. Several of these methods are quite simple and quick; others take more time and more planning.

- The most basic and immediate way to influence a government official is to call him or her on the telephone. Some officials are willing to spend a short time discussing a citizen's ideas about a local issue.
- Another fast and immediate means of influencing local government is through the use of electronic mail (e-mail). This is an especially good way to send a single message to several government officials at the same time.
- Citizens can approach government leaders through a simple letter sent through the mail. This method allows for a more thorough and detailed approach to a local problem.
- One or more citizens can speak about local issues at **council meetings.** Most town or city council members are inclined to take note of the views of any residents who involve themselves directly in local government.
- Individual residents or a group of citizens can lobby local officials to try to influence their views. By meeting with officials privately and discussing an issue with them, community

members can sometimes bring about significant change in local government policy.

- Finally, citizens can demand that their council members draft a referendum to change some existing local or state law. A **referendum** is a proposal that residents will vote to accept or reject in a local election. Similarly, in some communities, individual citizens may draft new laws themselves. These laws, called **citizens' initiatives,** must be written according to very detailed legal guidelines. Citizens then collect signatures from community residents who wish to support the initiative. If enough citizens sign, the initiative can appear on the voting ballot on election day. Though successful initiatives are quite rare, they do occasionally make it all the way from a citizen's pen to enacted law.

- Local management of such important matters as public education, zoning laws, and police protection continues a tradition of local independence and self-government that dates back to colonial America. The United States has a long history of citizens resisting centralized government and insisting on the right to govern themselves close to home. Hence, one can see across the country the importance the nation still puts on self-government. In matters as fundamental and wide-reaching as educating young people, protecting citizens' safety and freedom, and shaping growth and change in communities, the institutions of local government emphasize the importance of neighborhood and community.

- Democracy invites and benefits from direct involvement by citizens. Making direct contact with government officials is easiest and most likely at the local level. For this reason, it is important for interested citizens to recognize and utilize their own power to influence public policy.

 # Implications

To answer the question, "Why does all this matter?" or "What does it mean?," share the following insights with your child.

 # Fact Checker

To check that your child knows or can find the basic facts in this chapter, here is an activity based on knowledge of how local governments function and are structured.

Which services in the following list are *not* provided by local governments?

police protection	sanitation
overseeing of elections	creation of foreign policy
national defense	transportation
fire protection	social services for the poor
access to water	recreational facilities
maintenance of national parklands	cultural activities
management of public schools	establishment of post offices

Answers appear in the back, preceding the index.

The Big Question

The following question encourages your child to think critically rather than simply recall facts. If necessary, review the specific information from the preceding pages that will help your child make the necessary inferences to come up with a reasonable answer.

It could be argued that local government affects the personal lives of individual citizens even more than the federal government or state governments. However, many more people vote in national and state elections than in local elections. When local officials are elected, especially in small towns, many people don't bother to vote, and many do not even know the names of their local elected officials. How do you explain this fact?

Suggested Answer

Much more media attention is given to federal elections and to state elections. Candidates on the national and state levels have much more money to spend on campaigning and publicity. The issues addressed by national and state government seem bigger and more important, even though they may affect our personal lives less than issues addressed by local government.

Skills Practice

The following activities give your child practice in applying the skills basic to social studies. For some of the activities, your child may need to review the information in the preceding pages.

WRITING AN EXPLANATION

This activity gives your child practice in explaining in writing a complex idea so that another person can understand it. Students are often asked to do this in order to answer essay questions on written tests.

In one paragraph, explain how the three types of municipal government are structured: the mayor-council form, the council-manager form, and the commission form. The purpose of your paragraph is simply to explain—not to point out comparisons or contrasts or to make evaluations. Make sure your paragraph is as clear as possible.

Suggested Answer

In the mayor-council form of municipal government, the voters elect a mayor and members of a city council. Heads of city departments are appointed by the mayor. In the council-manager form of municipal government, voters elect members of a city council. The members of the council hire a city manager, who in turn appoints heads of the various town or city departments. The council also appoints a mayor, but he or she has only limited powers. In the commission form, voters elect a board of commissioners that includes the police, fire, parks, finance, and public works commissioners. One of the commissioners also has the title of mayor, but the mayor performs only ceremonial functions.

Evaluating Your Child's Skills: In order to complete this activity successfully, your child must be able to select the most basic facts from several passages and incorporate them into a simple explanation. Your child must also be able to write clearly. If necessary, guide your child back to the chart at the beginning of the chapter, and have him or her "translate" the chart into words.

Top of the Class

Children interested in delving more deeply into the topics covered in this chapter can choose one or both of the following activities. They may do the activities for their own satisfaction or report on what they have done to show that they have been seriously considering the structure and functioning of local governments.

RESEARCH: YOUR LOCAL GOVERNMENT

Suggest to your child that he or she find out the form of local government for your city or town and the names of the most important officials.

Do you know the form of your local government? Do you know the people at the head of your local government? Use a search engine on the Internet to find out the answers to these questions. Start your search by typing in the name of your city or town as a key word. Choose one or two of your local officials to find out more about. What qualifies this official to hold his or her position? What are his or her policies? Do you agree with them?

GETTING INVOLVED

Suggest that your child pick one of the ways mentioned in this chapter to make his or her voice heard in local government.

Is there an issue you would like to take up with an official in your local government? For example, are you dissatisfied with or do you have suggestions for improving your school system, traffic system, or recreational facilities? Write a letter or e-mail to the appropriate official who would handle your issue. First, you might want to attend the meeting of a community or neighborhood group or a council meeting to find out what issues are currently being discussed or debated in your locality.

CHAPTER 11
Governments of the World

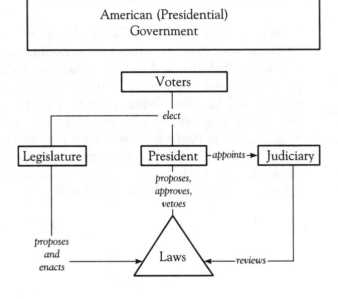

American (Presidential) Government

Voters

elect

Legislature   President   —*appoints*→   Judiciary

proposes, approves, vetoes

proposes and enacts →   Laws   ←*reviews*—

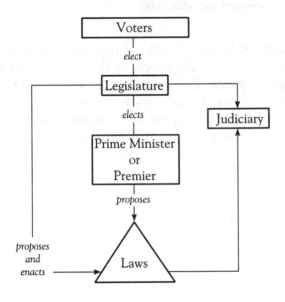

British (Parliamentary) Government

Voters

elect

Legislature

elects

Prime Minister or Premier   Judiciary

proposes

proposes and enacts →   Laws

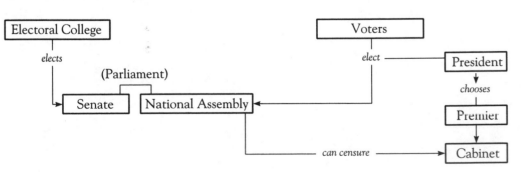

The French Presidential System

Electoral College

elects

(Parliament)

Senate   National Assembly   ←   Voters

elect —   President

chooses

Premier

can censure →   Cabinet

These diagrams provide an overview of the structures and functions of five national governments.

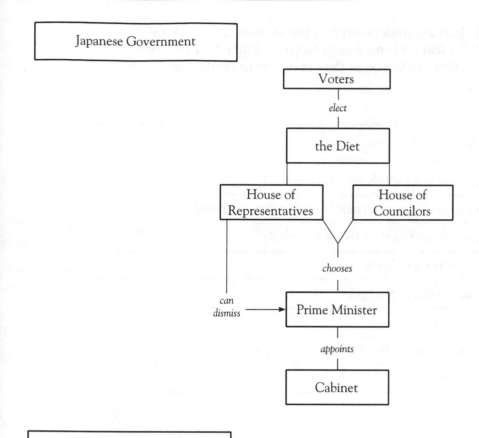

Japanese Government

Voters

elect

the Diet

House of Representatives

House of Councilors

chooses

can dismiss →

Prime Minister

appoints

Cabinet

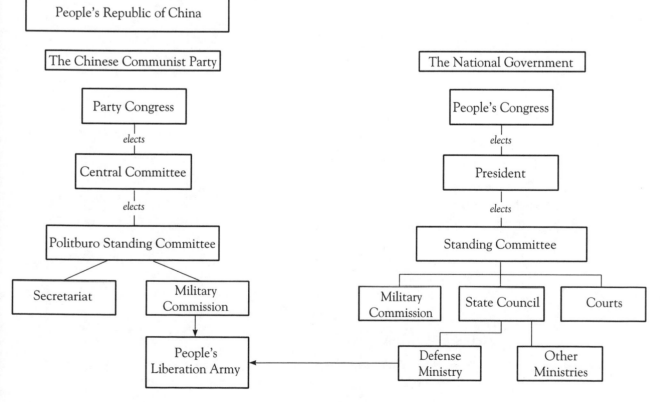

People's Republic of China

The Chinese Communist Party

Party Congress

elects

Central Committee

elects

Politburo Standing Committee

Secretariat

Military Commission

People's Liberation Army

The National Government

People's Congress

elects

President

elects

Standing Committee

Military Commission

State Council

Courts

Defense Ministry

Other Ministries

121

Word Power

The words on the following chart are underscored in the section called "What Your Child Needs to Know." Explain their meanings to your child either before going over the information in that section or as they come up in reading or discussion.

Word	Definition
inherited	received a title from someone who has died
intellectuals	people who spend most of their time thinking and studying
merging	joining two things together to form a whole
prominent	important; very easily seen
rural	in the countryside; not urban
steadfastly	firmly and without change
surrendering	admitting that you are beaten in a battle or contest
unanimous	agreed upon by all

What Your Child Needs to Know

You may choose to use the following text in several different ways, depending on your child's strengths and preferences. You might read the passage aloud; you might read it to yourself and then paraphrase it for your child; or you might ask your child to read the material along with you or on his or her own.

Houses of Parliament, London

THE UNITED STATES AND THE WORLD

In the first ten chapters of this book, we have examined the way government works in the United States of America. It is important, also, for Americans to become familiar with the structures and functions of governments in other nations. In addition to broadening our knowledge about the world as a whole, learning about other nations' systems of government helps us gain an even richer understanding of our own government. This final chapter provides information on the governments of four nations, as well as on the three economic systems that underlie those governments.

GREAT BRITAIN

The government of Great Britain is, like the government of the United States, a democracy. Unlike the United States, Great Britain has a monarchy, but the king or queen has no political power whatsoever. Britain's monarch serves ceremonial purposes only, but he or she is a powerful symbol of the unity of the nation.

The British Constitution

The British constitution is the basis for the government of Great Britain, yet only a few parts of that constitution have been written down. These written portions include other separate documents such as the English Bill of Rights, the Magna Carta, certain court decisions from the last several hundred years, and laws passed by the British legislature, known as Parliament. The rest of the British constitution's subject matter is not recorded on paper; instead, it has become part of the "fabric" of Britain's tradition. For example, for many generations, a **prime minister** has served as the chief executive of the British government. Yet nowhere is it noted officially that this should be the case.

The British system of government allows the constitution to be changed with relative ease. Parliament simply needs to vote to overturn earlier laws or practices. Consequently, the British government has been able to change and adapt over the centuries without a complicated amendment process.

Parliament and the Ministers

Britain's government does not separate power between legislative and executive officials. Yet, like the U.S. Congress, Britain's Parliament is bicameral (see Chapter 1), composed of the House of Commons and the House of Lords.

The House of Commons has 651 members of Parliament who are elected to five-year terms. This group creates the laws and policies that govern the nation. Members propose policies, debate each policy proposal, and then send it to one of eight standing committees. The committee irons out the policy's details and sends the proposal back to the House of Commons for a vote. The proposal passes into law if a majority of the House votes for it.

The House of Lords has far less power than the House of Commons. For example, the House of Lords does not even vote on whether a proposed law should pass. Though the House of Lords may veto a law passed by the House of Commons, the House of Commons has the power to override that veto and pass its own law anyway. The House of Lords is made up of twelve hundred members, most of whom are members of Britain's aristocracy. In fact, about 75 percent of the members of the House of Lords <u>inherited</u> their positions from their ancestors. The others have been awarded membership in the House of Lords for outstanding achievement or service to their country. Because members of the House of Lords are not elected, they are able to serve an important function in the British Parliament as a whole. That is, they have the freedom to debate policy with complete frankness and thoughtfulness, without worrying about pleasing or alienating voters. This freedom allows the House of Lords to act as watchdogs in the British Parliament.

The prime minister and other **ministers** make up the executive branch of the British government. Yet each of these officials is also a member of Parliament, the legislative branch of the government. In fact, the leader of the majority party in the House of Commons becomes the prime minister. That individual then appoints ministers (most of them also from the majority party in the House of Commons) to serve in the cabinet as the heads of various executive departments. This <u>merging</u> of the legislative and executive branches contrasts vividly with the structure of the American government.

Political Parties

For nearly a century, Great Britain has been dominated by one or the other of two political parties—the **Labour Party** and the **Conservative Party.** In general, the Labour Party is favored by members of Britain's strong labor unions and other members of the nation's working class. On the other hand, Britain's middle and upper classes tend to support the Conservative Party. Both parties are represented in the British Parliament. The majority party in the House of Commons is commonly referred to as *the government.* The minority party is referred to as *the opposition.* The majority party must maintain the support of a majority of members in the House of Commons. If the majority party loses this support, it must resign its leadership. At that point, the British Parliament is com-

pletely dissolved, and the nation votes for a completely new Parliament.

Local Government

The national government of Great Britain controls all local governments across the nation. These local governments supervise roads and transportation, public education, police and fire protection, and public health services.

FRANCE

Like the United States and Great Britain, France has a democratic government. Yet its government differs from each of those two in significant ways. The current French government, known as the **Fifth Republic,** has been in power since a new constitution was adopted in 1958. The Fifth Republic was established after a difficult period between 1946 and 1958. During these twelve years, dozens of political parties competed for power, and the French government changed twenty-seven times. The current constitution stabilized the nation by requiring that the government contain a strong president and a less powerful legislature.

The Executive Branch

Until 1958, the office of **president** carried little influence or power in France. The president appeared at public ceremonies but had little to do with actually governing the nation. In the Fifth Republic, the president is the most powerful position in the most important part of the nation's democratic government—the executive branch.

The French president—the only nationally elected official in the country—is elected to a seven-year term. The president possesses several important powers. The president does or can (1) make treaties with other nations; (2) appoint other government officials; (3) supervise the departments that control the French military; (4) issue a referendum to the nation's citizens, when necessary, to change governmental policy dramatically and immediately.

Appointed by the president, the French **premier** serves as the link between the president and the legislature. The premier appoints several leaders, called *ministers,* who form the executive cabinet. The cabinet's purpose is to help guide the president's policies through the **French Parliament.**

The French Parliament

In France, as in Great Britain, Parliament consists of a lower and an upper house. Both houses meet each October for a two-month session and each April for a three-month session. As its part-time schedule shows, the French Parliament has far less power than the executive branch. France's constitution grants the French Parliament the power to create laws and policies relating to national defense, civil rights, and police procedures. However, all other policies and laws are generated and passed by the executive branch without Parliament's approval.

Voters in France elect the 577 members of the **National Assembly,** Parliament's lower house. National Assembly members serve five-year terms and hold more power than those of the Senate, as the upper house is called. The Senate's 321 members, chosen by an electoral college for nine-year terms, have little real power except in stalling or delaying the final vote on legislation.

Political Parties

One of the aims of the governmental reforms of 1958 was to reduce the number of political parties in France by merging two or more parties. Today, a handful of major parties exists, grouped and labeled as either **left-wing** or **right-wing** parties. The left wing includes the Socialist Party and the Communist Party. The Gaullist Party and the Union for French Democracy are two prominent right-wing parties. Each of the major political parties is represented in the French Parliament. In addition, several smaller parties continue to exercise some influence.

Local Government

France is divided into ninety-six territories, known as **departments.** Each of these departments is represented by a commissioner in the nation's capitol, Paris. Though these commissioners have gained a small measure of power in the last few decades, French departments are still governed largely by the central government.

JAPAN

The governments of Japan and Great Britain are remarkably similar in organization and function. The current Japanese system of government has been in place since the end of World War II.

The Japanese Constitution

Japan ended World War II in 1945 by surrendering to the United States. In the years that followed, the U.S. government helped Japan recover and rebuild itself as a democratic nation. The American government supervised the writing of a new Japanese constitution, which was put into practice in 1947. Whereas, before the war, Japan had been run by powerful military and industrial leaders and the emperor had been regarded as a god, the new constitution stated that the Japanese people, "acting through . . . duly elected representatives," would hold governmental power in their own hands. It also stated that the emperor would have no "powers related to government."

Instead of designing Japan's new government to resemble the American government, the Americans who wrote Japan's constitution structured it more like the British government. They did this because Great Britain and Japan shared certain traditions—most notably, a monarch.

The Diet and the Cabinet

Japan's bicameral legislature, known as the **National Diet,** is composed of the **House of Representatives** (the lower house) and the **House of Councilors** (the upper house). Like the upper houses of the British and French parliaments, Japan's House of Councilors has little real governing power. However, its members, elected for six-year terms, serve the valuable purpose of debating proposed legislation calmly and thoroughly before it can be enacted into law.

True governing power rests with the 512 members of the House of Representatives, each of whom is elected for a four-year term. The lower house of the Japanese legislature generates budget policy and treaties. It also provides the nation with its prime minister. As in Great Britain, the leader of the majority party in the House of Representatives becomes prime minister. This leader then appoints the members of the cabinet, half of whom must be members of the National Diet.

The cabinet's twelve members are the leaders of a dozen governmental agencies or departments—the Ministry of Finance, the Ministry of Labor, the

Ministry of Foreign Affairs, the Ministry of Forestry, and so on. These twelve individuals are expected to make decisions as a <u>unanimous</u> team. If a cabinet member takes a different position from the rest, that member is expected to resign the cabinet post or risk dismissal by the prime minister. This system is partly responsible for an unusually high rate of change in the membership of the cabinet from year to year. At other times, cabinet officials are called to be examined and questioned by committees of the National Diet. There they face fiery cross-examination by members of the Diet's opposition parties.

The Supreme Court

Like the U.S. Constitution, the constitution of Japan provides for a Supreme Court that has the power to decide whether or not laws are constitutional. But the Japanese Supreme Court is not nearly as active as that of the United States. Since the adoption of the Japanese constitution, only a few laws have been declared unconstitutional.

Political Parties

Three major political parties dominate the Japanese government. Established in 1955, the **Liberal Democratic Party (LDP)** is by far most powerful. As its name implies, this party promotes the free enterprise system and the growth of Japan's economy. Two opposition parties, the **Social Democratic Party** (formerly known as the Japanese Socialist Party) and the **Japanese Communist Party,** also hold seats in the National Diet.

Local Government

Japan is divided into forty-seven territories, called **prefectures.** Each of these prefectures is supervised by a governor and an assembly. In addition, each prefecture is divided into smaller political units, such as *shi* (the city), *machi* or *cho* (the town), and *mura* or *son* (the village). Mayors and assemblies administrate these districts.

THE PEOPLE'S REPUBLIC OF CHINA

For a little over a half century, China has been ruled by the **Chinese Communist Party.** Chinese communist leaders based certain aspects of their government on the totalitarian government of the former Soviet Union; they made other aspects uniquely Chinese. (A **totalitarian** government is one in which one person or a small group of people hold absolute power.) Despite the number of nations in Eastern Europe that rejected communism in the 1980s and 1990s (including the Soviet Union), China remains <u>steadfastly</u> communist to this day.

The Chinese Communist Party and the National Government

It surprises many people to learn that fewer than 5 percent of China's citizens are members of the Chinese Communist Party. Despite its small membership, this political organization has absolute control over the Chinese government, as well as over economic institutions, cultural institutions, and the Chinese people. The highest official in the Chinese Communist Party is the **general secretary.**

It is hard for outsiders to get a clear idea of how power really works in the People's Republic of China. This is partly because the Chinese Communist Party and the government are two separate organizations, and the relationship between the two is not always obvious. For example, some members of the Chinese Communist Party hold important positions in China's national government, yet the party's general secretary is not always a government official. In fact, **Deng Xiaoping**—China's most important leader during much of the 1970s and 1980s—held no official position in either the national government or in the Chinese Communist Party. To make things even more confusing, in 1982, China adopted two separate constitutions— one for the Chinese Communist Party and one for the national government.

Party Organization

The **National Party Congress,** composed of fifteen hundred to two thousand delegates, is supposedly the highest governing body of the Chinese Communist Party. Rather than create party policy, however, the National Party Congress serves as a "rubber stamp" for the policies of the party's leaders. The delegates elect two hundred to three hundred members to serve on the party's **Central Committee,** which in turn elects about twenty party leaders to the party's political bureau, the **Politburo.** The Politburo selects from its members six top party leaders to serve on the **Politburo's Standing Committee,** which appoints members of the **Secretariat**—the organization that implements party policies.

National Government Organization

The **National People's Congress** is the "highest organ of state power," according to the 1982 constitution, but, in reality, it has little power. It selects China's president, vice president, and premier, but these people also have little power. A body called the **State Council,** comparable to a cabinet or council of ministers in other countries, is supposedly responsible to the National People's Congress. However, it is actually controlled by the Chinese Communist Party's Politburo, and most of the State Council leaders are also leaders in the party. The State Council's functions are to make decisions regarding legislation and the budget and to make sure the party's policies are followed.

Political Parties

Despite the absolute power of the Chinese Communist Party, the People's Republic of China does allow eight additional political parties to exist. These parties have small memberships composed of students, intellectuals, and some middle-class citizens. The Chinese government expects these parties to function under the supervision of the Chinese Communist Party.

Local Government

Since the 1980s, free elections have been permitted in rural villages. Citizens of these small communities have elected their own leaders without interference by government or party officials. The government of the United States has praised this small step toward political freedom and democracy. However, similar elections have not occurred in larger towns or cities.

WORLD ECONOMIC SYSTEMS

The phrase *economic system* refers to the way people make, buy, and sell things in a particular country. The three economic systems that exist in the world today are capitalism, socialism, and communism. But before discussing each of these systems, some terms need to be defined.

goods: things that are made or grown, bought, and sold (wheat, cars, clothing, books, airplanes)

labor: people who work in order to produce and sell goods (fruit pickers, factory workers, computer programmers, newspaper reporters, and so on)

capital: whatever is needed, in addition to labor, in order to produce and sell goods (money and machinery, for example)

means of production: labor and capital plus natural resources (land, coal, oil, and so on)

management: people in control of the means of production (anyone who owns a business, from a manufacturer of heavy farm equipment to the owner of a small store)

profit: money made when something is sold, after subtracting costs for labor and other expenses

consumers: people who buy goods

Capitalism

The central idea on which capitalism is based is that capital and natural resources are owned, for the most part, by private individuals and companies—not by the government. In a capitalist economy, any person may start a business and try to make a profit by selling goods he or she thinks consumers will want at a price that is the same as or lower than that of other businesses—the **competition.** Profits are also increased by keeping expenses down. The less money management has to pay out, the more money is left over in the end. No one tells business owners what they can or must produce or sell. Free choice, therefore, is another main idea on which capitalism is based. Another term for *capitalism,* in fact, is **free enterprise.**

Some problems arise in a capitalist system. First of all, one way of keeping expenses down is to pay labor as little as possible. This creates a situation that encourages management to treat labor unfairly and in which a small segment of the population—owners of big businesses—is very rich while a large number of people have much less. There may even be people who cannot afford the necessities of life such as food, housing, and medical care. In order to combat these problems, capitalist countries, such as the United States, impose certain government regulations on business. For example, the government enacts **antitrust legislation**—laws preventing one business from putting all its competition out of business and thus controlling an entire industry, charging whatever it likes for its products; it requires businesses to pay at least a minimum wage to its employees; and it makes sure that employees have safe and healthy conditions in which to work. The U.S. government also supports social programs such as Medicare and Medicaid, social security, low-rent public housing, and food stamps to make sure that people are not deprived of the basic necessities of life. There is ongoing debate in the United States over whether the government does too much or too little in this respect. There are still people who live in poverty, yet some believe that more government regulation and more social welfare programs will create a "welfare state" and be a threat to our system of free enterprise, so closely associated with democracy.

Socialism

The central idea on which socialism is based is that land and labor are publicly owned, in other words, owned by the government. A socialist economic system operates on the belief that capitalism's focus on profit and competition contributes to an unfair division between rich and poor and encourages management to treat labor unfairly. Under socialism, goods and wealth supposedly are distributed equally among all citizens. In addition, under socialism, the government determines what goods will be produced and at what prices they will be sold.

Some nations employ socialist economic ideas only in specific industries. For example, the British government goes much further with government regulation and social programs than does the United States. The government of Great Britain owns its railroad and airline systems; coal, steel, gas, and electric power industries; and its system for medical care. By applying socialist ideas to these particular areas, the government sees to it that all citizens get the basic necessities of life. In other areas, Great Britain adheres to a free enterprise system.

Problems that have been cited as being inherent in a socialist economic system are that it makes peo-

ple too dependent on the government and that the social programs administered by the government are not free—citizens are highly taxed to pay for them.

Communism

The central ideas of communism are similar to those of socialism, but there are two important differences. First, in a socialist nation, citizens can vote the government, which controls the means of production, out of power. In a communist economy, only one political party—the Communist Party—is permitted to hold power. The citizens have no choice in who will control the means of production and how the means of production will be managed. Second, under communism, the government controls all areas of the economy, not only selected ones. The government, not business owners or consumers, decide how natural resources will be used, what goods will be produced, and at what prices they will be sold. In the early years of the twenty-first century, only a few nations still use this economic system. The U.S.S.R. (Union of Soviet Socialist Republics) broke up at the end of the twentieth century and abandoned communism for a capitalist system.

 *Implications*

To answer the question, "Why does all this matter?" or "What does it mean?," share the following insights with your child.

- **Government leaders, political party leaders, and other national leaders hold varying degrees of power in different nations.** In Great Britain, for example, the queen possesses absolutely no governmental power. However, it would be naïve and inaccurate to say that she is not a national leader or that she has no power or influence across Great Britain. Most British citizens respect the queen and other members of the royal family as leaders of their society. Nonetheless, in contrast to the British prime minister, the queen has virtually no political power whatsoever. The emperor of Japan holds a similar position in Japanese society. It is important to understand exactly what powers and functions each national leader actually possesses.

- **An economic system carries with it more ideas than just those about money, buying, and selling.** Capitalism, socialism, and communism are political and social philosophies as well as economic systems. Each says something about human nature, the relationship of human beings to each other, and the relation-

ships between individuals and the government under which they live. For example, capitalism assumes that the desire for profit stimulates business in a healthy way, whereas communism takes the view that the profit motive encourages private business to exploit both labor and consumers if given the chance. Moreover, both socialism and communism see a greater need for government control of individuals than does capitalism.

Fact Checker

To check that your child knows or can find the basic facts in this chapter, here is a fill-in activity based on knowledge of how different governments of the world function and are structured.

Following is a list of characteristics of the governments of Great Britain, France, Japan, and China. On the line before each characteristic, write the name of the nation or nations the characteristic applies to. Some characteristics apply to more than one of the four nations.

1. _Japan, Great Britain, France_ Bicameral legislature
2. _Great Britain China_ Totalitarian government
3. _Great Britain_ Two major parties
4. _France China_ Only one party
5. _Great Britain Japan_ Three major parties
6. _China_ Free elections only in small villages
7. _Japan China_ Communism
8. _Great Britain, France_ Capitalism (free enterprise)
9. _France_ Several major parties and several smaller parties
10. _Great Britain, Japan_ Majority leader in lower house of the legislature is prime minister.
11. _France, Great Britain, France_ Laws about anything but national defense, civil rights, and police procedures generated and passed by executive branch without approval of Parliament.
12. _Japan, France_ Twelve cabinet members must make unanimous decisions.

Answers appear in the back, preceding the index.

? The Big Questions

The following questions encourage your child to think critically rather than simply recall facts. If necessary, review the specific information from the preceding pages that will help your child make the necessary inferences to come up with reasonable answers.

1. In the United States, Great Britain, France, and Japan, democracy and capitalism work successfully, yet the way the governments of these four countries function and are structured differ in several ways. What conclusion can you draw from the fact that these four nations are democratic but different?
2. The original idea of communism was that each person would work hard and do his or her best, but no one would make more money than anyone else. Instead, everyone would be given enough to fulfill his or her needs. This would eliminate the gap between rich people and poor people that creates major problems in capitalist countries. Why do you think that communism seems to require a totalitarian form of government? Why can't it work in a democracy? Can you think of ways to end poverty in a democratic nation?

Suggested Answers

1. *One conclusion that can certainly be drawn is that there is no one way to run a democratic government. Different methods seem to work. Perhaps each democratic nation has developed the method that is best for its particular way of life.*
2. *Accept any reasonable answer. One possible answer would be that, by nature, individuals want to reap the benefits of their own work and talents, that they do not want to share with people who are not able to produce as much. Given individual liberties, even people with charitable impulses will keep most of what they produce for themselves.*

Skills Practice

The following activity gives your child practice in applying skills basic to social studies. Your child may need to review the information in the preceding pages in order to complete the activity.

WRITING A COMPARE-AND-CONTRAST ESSAY

This activity gives your child practice in writing a multiple-paragraph essay in which he or she points out both similarities (comparisons) and differences (contrasts) between two things or ideas. Before your child begins, you might go over the basic rules for structuring an essay:

- **Begin with an introductory paragraph that states the main idea of the essay. Each of the other paragraphs in the essay should directly support that main idea, or thesis statement.**
- **Include in each subsequent paragraph a sentence that states the main idea of the paragraph (the topic sentence). Each of the other sentences in the paragraph should directly support the topic sentence with facts or examples.**
- **End with a concluding paragraph that sums up the other paragraphs, emphasizes the main idea of the essay, or tells why the ideas expressed in the essay are important.**

In an essay of four paragraphs, compare and contrast the governments of two of the countries described in this chapter: Great Britain, France, Japan, and China. The first paragraph will be your introduction, in which you state the main idea of your essay. The second paragraph should tell how the two governments you've chosen are similar, and the third should show how they are different. The fourth paragraph should be your conclusion—perhaps a summary of the other three.

Answer

Your child's essay should make the point that the two governments are similar in some ways and different in others. The essay should point out several similarities and differences that are mentioned in the chapter.

Evaluating Your Child's Skills: In order to complete this activity successfully, your child must have a basic understanding of how to structure an essay. If he or she needs help, you might suggest a thesis statement and two topic sentences to use. Thesis statement: The governments of Great Britain and Japan are similar in some ways but differ in some ways as well. Topic sentence for first paragraph: The governments of Great Britain and Japan are similar in the way they are structured. Topic sentence for second paragraph: The governments of Great Britain and Japan are different in some of the ways they function. The conclusion might summarize and make the point that both countries are democratic nations.

 # Top of the Class

Children interested in delving more deeply into the topics covered in this chapter can choose one or both of the following activities. They may do the activities for their own satisfaction or report on what they have done to show that they have been seriously considering the similarities and differences among several nations of the world.

RESEARCH: WORLD LEADERS

Suggest to your child that he or she find out something about the most important leaders of the four nations described in this chapter.

You have learned the basic facts about the way the governments of Great Britain, France, Japan, and China are structured and function. But do you know who the leaders of these nations are? Use a search engine on the Internet to find out who they are and a little bit of general information about them. Begin your search by typing in the name of the country you want to learn more about. Find out who is the prime minister or major leader of the country. What ideas and qualities is this person known for? After you complete this activity, you will be familiar with the names you see in newspapers and hear about on TV or radio news programs.

BOOKS TO READ

Suggest that your child read one or more of the following fiction or nonfiction books and respond by offering an oral or written critique.

Buck, Pearl. *The Big Wave.* HarperCollins, 1973. The courage of a young Japanese boy whose family and home are lost in a tidal wave. Fiction set in Japan.

Gilbert, Adrian. *The French Revolution* (*Revolution!* series) Thomson Learning, 1995.

Kent, Deborah. *Beijing* (*Cities of the World* series). Children's Press, 1996. History of Beijing and details about how people live there now.

Smith, Nigel. *The Houses of Parliament* (*Great Buildings* series) Raintree Steck-Vaughn, 1997. A history of the British Houses of Parliament plus basic information about the British form of government.

Sproule, Anna. *Great Britain: The Land and Its People.* Silver Burdett, 1991.

Tames, Richard. *Exploration into Japan* (*Exploration* series). Dillon, 1996. A brief history of Japan.

Tan, Amy. *The Moon Lady.* Macmillan, 1992. A grandmother in the United States reminisces about growing up in China. Fiction adapted for children from Tan's novel *The Joy Luck Club.*

Waterlow, Julia. *China* (*Country Insights* series) Raintree Steck-Vaughn, 1997. Comparison of life in a large city and a small village in China.

APPENDIX A

Presidents of the United States

No.	President (birth and death dates)	Term(s)	Party	Vice President(s)
1	George Washington (1732–1799)	1789–1797		John Adams
2	John Adams (1735–1826)	1797–1801	Federalist	Thomas Jefferson
3	Thomas Jefferson (1743–1826)	1801–1809	Democratic-Republican	Aaron Burr George Clinton
4	James Madison (1751–1836)	1809–1817	Democratic-Republican	George Clinton Elbridge Gerry
5	James Monroe (1758–1831)	1817–1825	Democratic-Republican	Daniel D. Tompkins
6	John Quincy Adams (1767–1848)	1825–1829	Democratic-Republican	John C. Calhoun
7	Andrew Jackson (1767–1845)	1829–1837	Democratic	John C. Calhoun Martin Van Buren
8	Martin Van Buren (1782–1862)	1837–1841	Democratic	Richard M. Johnson
9	William H. Harrison (1773–1841)	1841	Whig	John Tyler
10	John Tyler (1790–1862)	1841–1845	Whig	None
11	James K. Polk (1795–1849)	1845–1849	Democratic	George M. Dallas
12	Zachary Taylor (1784–1850)	1849–1850	Whig	Millard Fillmore
13	Millard Fillmore (1800–1874)	1850–1853	Whig	None
14	Franklin Pierce (1804–1869)	1853–1857	Democratic	William R. King
15	James Buchanan (1791–1868)	1857–1861	Democratic	John C. Breckinridge

No.	President (birth and death dates)	Term(s)	Party	Vice President(s)
16	Abraham Lincoln (1809–1865)	1861–1865	Republican	Hannibal Hamlin Andrew Johnson
17	Andrew Johnson (1808–1875)	1865–1869	Republican	None
18	Ulysses S. Grant (1822–1885)	1869–1877	Republican	Schuyler Colfax Henry Wilson
19	Rutherford B. Hayes (1822–1893)	1877–1881	Republican	William A. Wheeler
20	James A. Garfield (1831–1881)	1881	Republican	Chester A. Arthur
21	Chester A. Arthur (1830–1886)	1881–1885	Republican	None
22 24	Grover Cleveland (1837–1908)	1885–1889 1893–1897	Democratic	Thomas A. Hendricks Adlai E. Stevenson
23	Benjamin Harrison (1833–1901)	1889–1893	Republican	Levi P. Morton
25	William McKinley (1843–1901)	1897–1901	Republican	Garret Hobart Theodore Roosevelt
26	Theodore Roosevelt (1858–1919)	1901–1909	Republican	Charles W. Fairbanks
27	William H. Taft (1857–1930)	1909–1913	Republican	James S. Sherman
28	Woodrow Wilson (1856–1924)	1913–1921	Democratic	Thomas R. Marshall
29	Warren G. Harding (1865–1923)	1921–1923	Republican	Calvin Coolidge
30	Calvin Coolidge (1872–1933)	1923–1929	Republican	Charles G. Dawes
31	Herbert C. Hoover (1874–1964)	1929–1933	Republican	Charles Curtis
32	Franklin D. Roosevelt (1882–1945)	1933–1945	Democrat	John N. Garner Henry A. Wallace Harry S Truman
33	Harry S Truman (1884–1972)	1945–1953	Democrat	Alben W. Barkley

No.	President (birth and death dates)	Term(s)	Party	Vice President(s)
34	Dwight D. Eisenhower (1890–1969)	1953–1961	Republican	Richard M. Nixon
35	John F. Kennedy (1917–1963)	1961–1963	Democrat	Lyndon B. Johnson
36	Lyndon B. Johnson (1908–1973)	1963–1969	Democrat	Hubert H. Humphrey
37	Richard M. Nixon (1913–1994)	1969–1974	Republican	Spiro T. Agnew Gerald R. Ford
38	Gerald R. Ford (1913–)	1974–1977	Republican	Nelson A. Rockefeller
39	James E. Carter (1924–)	1977–1981	Democrat	Walter F. Mondale
40	Ronald W. Reagan (1911–)	1981–1989	Republican	George H. Bush
41	George H. Bush (1924–)	1989–1993	Republican	J. Danforth Quayle
42	William Jefferson Clinton (1946–)	1993–2001	Democrat	Albert Gore, Jr.
43	George W. Bush (1946–)	2001–	Republican	Richard B. Cheney

APPENDIX B

Preamble to the Constitution of the United States (1789)

We the People of the United States, in order to form a more perfect Union, establish Justice, insure domestic tranquility, provide for the common defense, promote the general Welfare, and secure the Blessing of Liberty to ourselves and our Posterity, do ordain and establish this Constitution for the United States of America.

Bill of Rights (1791)

Amendment 1. Freedom of Religion, Speech, Press, Assembly, and Petition

Congress shall make no law respecting an establishment of religion, or prohibiting the free exercise thereof; or abridging the freedom of speech, or of the press; or the right of the people peaceably to assemble, and to petition the government for a redress of grievances.

Amendment 2. Right to Keep Weapons

A well-regulated militia, being necessary to the security of a free state, the right of the people to keep and bear arms shall not be infringed.

Amendment 3. Protection Against Quartering Soldiers

No soldier shall, in time of peace, be quartered in any house, without the consent of the owner, nor in time of war, but in a manner prescribed by law.

Amendment 4. Freedom from Unreasonable Search and Seizure

The right of the people to be secure in their persons, house, papers, and effects, against unreasonable searches and seizures, shall not be violated, and no warrants shall issue, but upon probable cause, supported by oath or affirmation, and particularly describing the place to be searched, and the persons or things to be seized.

Amendment 5. Rights of Persons Accused of a Crime

No person shall be held to answer for a capital, or otherwise infamous, crime, unless on a presentment or indictment of a grand jury, except in cases arising in the land or naval forces, or in the militia, when in actual service in time of war or public danger; nor shall any person be subject for the same offense to be twice put in jeopardy of life or limb; nor shall be compelled in any criminal case to be a witness against himself, nor to be deprived of life, liberty, or property, without due process of law; nor shall private property be taken for public use, without just compensation.

Amendment 6. Right to a Jury Trial in Criminal Cases

In all criminal prosecutions, the accused shall enjoy the right to a speedy and public trial, by an impartial jury of the state and district wherein the crime shall have been committed, which district shall have been previously ascertained by law, and to be informed of the nature and cause of the accusation; to be confronted with the witnesses against him; to have compulsory process for obtaining witnesses in his favor, and to have the assistance of counsel for his defense.

Amendment 7. Right to a Jury Trial in Civil Cases

In suits at common law, where the value in controversy shall exceed twenty dollars, the right of trial by jury shall be preserved, and no fact tried by a jury shall be otherwise re-examined in any court of the United States than according to the rules of the common law.

Amendment 8. Protection from Unfair Fines and Punishment

Excessive bail should not be required, nor excessive fines imposed, nor cruel and unusual punishments inflicted.

Amendment 9. Other Rights of the People

The enumeration in the Constitution, of certain rights, shall not be construed to deny or disparage others retained by the people.

Amendment 10. Powers of the States and the People

The powers not delegated to the United States by the Constitution, nor prohibited by its states, are reserved to the states respectively, or to the people.

APPENDIX C

Declaration of Independence (1776)

When in the Course of human events it becomes necessary for one people to dissolve the political bands which have connected them and to assume among the powers of the earth the separate and equal station to which the Laws of Nature and of Nature's God entitle them, a decent respect to the opinions of mankind requires that they should declare the causes which impel them to the separation.

We hold these truths to be self-evident: that all men are created equal; that they are endowed by their Creator with certain unalienable Rights; that among these are Life, Liberty and the pursuit of Happiness; That to secure these rights, Governments are instituted among Men, deriving their just powers from the consent of the governed; That whenever any Form of Government becomes destructive of these ends, it is the Right of the People to alter or to abolish it, and to institute new Government, laying its foundation on such principles, and organizing its powers in such form, as to them shall seem most likely to effect their Safety and Happiness. Prudence, indeed, will dictate that Governments long established should not be changed for light and transient causes; and accordingly all experience hath shown that mankind are more disposed to suffer while evils are sufferable than to right themselves by abolishing the forms to which they are accustomed. But when a long train of abuses and usurpations, pursuing invariably the same Objects, evinces a design to reduce them under absolute Despotism, it is their right, it is their duty, to throw off such Government, and to provide new Guards for their future security. Such has been the patient sufferance of these Colonies; and such is now the necessity which constrains them to alter their former Systems of Government. The history of the present King of Great Britain is a history of repeated injuries and usurpations, all having in direct object the establishment of an absolute Tyranny over the States. To prove this, let Facts be submitted to a candid world.

He has refused his Assent to Laws the most wholesome and necessary for the public good.

He has forbidden his Governors to pass Laws of immediate and pressing importance, unless suspended in their operation till his Assent should be obtained; and when so suspended, he has utterly neglected to attend to them.

He has refused to pass other Laws for the accommodation of large districts of people, unless these people would relinquish the right of Representation in the Legislature, a right inestimable to them and formidable to tyrants only.

He has called together legislative bodies at places unusual, uncomfortable, and distant from the depositary of their public records, for the sole purpose of fatiguing them into compliance with his measures.

He has dissolved Representative Houses repeatedly, for opposing with manly firmness his invasions on the right of the people.

He has refused for a long time after such dissolutions to cause others to be elected, whereby the Legislative powers, incapable of Annihilation, have returned to the People at large for their exercise, the State remaining in the mean time exposed to all the dangers of invasions from without and convulsions within.

He has endeavored to prevent the population of these States; for that purpose obstructing the Laws for Naturalization of Foreigners, refusing to pass others to encourage their migration hither, and raising the conditions of new Appropriations of Lands.

He has obstructed the Administration of Justice, by refusing his Assent to Laws for establishing Judiciary powers.

He has made Judges dependent on his Will alone for the tenure of their offices, and the amount of their salaries.

He has erected a multitude of New Offices, and sent hither swarms of Officers to harass our people and eat out their substance.

He has kept among us, in times of peace, Standing Armies, without the Consent of our legislatures.

He has affected to render the Military independent of, and superior to, the Civil power.

He has combined with others to subject us to a jurisdiction foreign to our constitution and unacknowledged by our laws; giving his Assent to their Acts of pretended Legislation:

For quartering large bodies of armed troops among us;

For protecting them, by a mock Trial, from punishment for any murders which they should commit on the Inhabitants of these States;

For cutting off our Trade with parts of the world;

For imposing Taxes on us without our Consent;

For depriving us, in many cases, of the benefits of Trial by Jury;

For transporting us beyond Seas to be tried for pretended offenses;

For abolishing the free System of English Laws in a neighboring Province, establishing therein an Arbitrary government, and enlarging its boundaries, so as to render it at once an example and fit instrument for introducing the same absolute rule into these Colonies;

For taking away our Charters, abolishing our most valuable Laws, and altering, fundamentally, the Forms of our Governments;

For suspending our own Legislatures, and declaring themselves invested with Power to legislate for us in all cases whatsoever.

He has abdicated Government here, by declaring us out of his Protection and waging War against us.

He has plundered our seas, ravaged our Coasts, burned our towns, and destroyed the lives of our people.

He is at this time transporting large Armies of foreign Mercenaries to complete the works of death, desolation and tyranny, already begun with circumstances of Cruelty and perfidy scarcely paralleled in the most barbarous ages, and totally unworthy the Head of a civilized nation.

He has constrained our fellow Citizens taken on the high Seas to bear Arms against their Country, to become the executioners of their friends and Brethren, or to fall themselves by their Hands.

He has excited domestic insurrections amongst us, and has endeavored to bring on the inhabitants of our frontiers the merciless Indian Savages whose known rule of warfare is an undistinguished destruction of all ages, sexes, and conditions.

In every stage of these Oppressions We have Petitioned for Redress in the most humble terms. Our repeated Petitions have been answered only by repeated injury. A Prince whose character is thus marked by every act which may define a Tyrant is unfit to be the ruler of a free people.

Nor have We been wanting in attentions to our British Brethren. We have warned them from time to time of attempts by their legislature to extend an unwarrantable jurisdiction over us. We have reminded them of the circumstances of our emigration and settlement here. We have appealed to their native justice and magnanimity, and we have conjured them by the ties of our common kindred to disavow these usurpations, which would inevitably interrupt our connections and correspondence. They too have been deaf to the voice of justice and consanguinity. We must therefore acquiesce in the necessity which denounces our Separation and hold them, as we hold the rest of mankind, Enemies in War, in Peace Friends.

We, therefore, the Representatives of the United States of America in General Congress Assembled, appealing to the Supreme Judge of the world for the rectitude of our intentions, do in the Name and by the Authority of the good people of these Colonies, solemnly publish and declare that these United Colonies are and of right ought to be Free and Independent States; that they are Absolved from all Allegiance to the British Crown, and that all political connection between them and the State of Great Britain is and ought to be totally dissolved, and that as Free and Independent States, they have full Power to levy War, conclude Peace, contract Alliance, establish Commerce, and to do all other Acts and Things which Independent States may of right do.

And for the support of this Declaration, with a firm reliance on the protection of Divine Providence, we mutually pledge to each other our Lives, our Fortunes, and our sacred Honor.

APPENDIX D

Members of the U.S. Supreme Court

Chief Justices

Name	State	Term
John Jay	New York	1789–1795
John Rutledge	South Carolina	1795
Oliver Ellsworth	Connecticut	1796–1800
John Marshall	Virginia	1801–1835
Roger B. Taney	Maryland	1836–1864
Salmon P. Chase	Ohio	1864–1873
Morrison R. Waite	Ohio	1874–1888
Melville W. Fuller	Illinois	1888–1910
Edward D. White	Louisiana	1910–1921
William H. Taft	Connecticut	1921–1930
Charles E. Hughes	New York	1930–1941
Harlan F. Stone	New York	1941–1946
Frederick M. Vinson	Kentucky	1946–1953
Earl Warren	California	1953–1969
Warren E. Burger	Virginia	1969–1986
William H. Rehnquist	Arizona	1986–

Associate Justices

Name	State	Term
James Wilson	Pennsylvania	1789–1798
John Rutledge	South Carolina	1790–1791
William Cushing	Massachusetts	1790–1810
John Blair	Virginia	1790–1796
James Iredell	North Carolina	1790–1799
Thomas Johnson	Maryland	1792–1793

Name	State	Term
William Paterson	New Jersey	1793–1806
Samuel Chase	Maryland	1796–1811
Bushrod Washington	Virginia	1799–1829
Alfred Moore	North Carolina	1800–1804
William Johnson	South Carolina	1804–1834
Brockholst Livingston	New York	1807–1823
Thomas Todd	Kentucky	1807–1826
Gabriel Duval	Maryland	1811–1835
Joseph Story	Massachusetts	1812–1845
Smith Thompson	New York	1823–1843
Robert Trimble	Kentucky	1826–1828
John McLean	Ohio	1830–1861
Henry Baldwin	Pennsylvania	1830–1844
James M. Wayne	Georgia	1835–1867
Philip P. Barbour	Virginia	1836–1841
John Catron	Tennessee	1837–1865
John McKinley	Alabama	1837–1852
Peter V. Daniel	Virginia	1841–1860
Samuel Nelson	New York	1845–1872
Levi Woodbury	New Hampshire	1845–1851
Robert C. Grier	Pennsylvania	1846–1870
Benjamin R. Curtis	Massachusetts	1851–1857
John A. Campbell	Alabama	1853–1861
Nathan Clifford	Maine	1858–1881
Noah H. Swayne	Ohio	1862–1881
Samuel F. Miller	Iowa	1862–1890
David Davis	Illinois	1862–1877
Stephen J. Field	California	1863–1897
William Strong	Pennsylvania	1870–1880
Joseph P. Bradley	New Jersey	1870–1892
Ward Hunt	New York	1872–1882
John M. Harlan	Kentucky	1877–1911

Name	State	Term
William B. Woods	Georgia	1880–1887
Stanley Matthews	Ohio	1881–1889
Horace Gray	Massachusetts	1882–1902
Samuel Blatchford	New York	1882–1893
Lucius Q. C. Lamar	Mississippi	1888–1893
David J. Brewer	Kansas	1889–1910
Henry B. Brown	Michigan	1890–1906
George Shiras, Jr.	Pennsylvania	1892–1903
Howell E. Jackson	Tennessee	1893–1895
Edward D. White*	Louisiana	1894–1910
Rufus W. Peckham	New York	1895–1909
Joseph McKenna	California	1898–1925
Oliver W. Holmes	Massachusetts	1902–1932
William R. Day	Ohio	1903–1922
William H. Moody	Massachusetts	1906–1910
Horace H. Lurton	Tennessee	1909–1914
Charles E. Hughes*	New York	1910–1916
Willis Van Devanter	Wyoming	1910–1937
Joseph R. Lamar	Georgia	1910–1916
Mahlon Pitney	New Jersey	1912–1922
James C. McReynolds	Tennessee	1914–1941
Louis D. Brandeis	Massachusetts	1916–1939
John H. Clarke	Ohio	1916–1922
George Sutherland	Utah	1922–1938
Pierce Butler	Minnesota	1923–1939
Edward T. Sanford	Tennessee	1923–1930
Harlan F. Stone*	New York	1925–1941
Owen J. Roberts	Pennsylvania	1930–1945
Benjamin N. Cardozo	New York	1932–1938
Hugo L. Black	Alabama	1937–1971
Stanley F. Reed	Kentucky	1938–1957
Felix Frankfurter	Massachusetts	1939–1962

Name	State	Term
William O. Douglas	Connecticut	1939–1975
Frank Murphy	Michigan	1940–1949
James F. Byrnes	South Carolina	1941–1942
Robert H. Jackson	Pennsylvania	1941–1954
Wiley B. Rutledge	Iowa	1943–1949
Harold H. Burton	Ohio	1945–1958
Tom C. Clark	Texas	1949–1967
Sherman Minton	Indiana	1949–1956
John M. Harlan	New York	1955–1971
William J. Brennan, Jr.	New Jersey	1956–1990
Charles E. Whittaker	Missouri	1957–1962
Potter Stewart	Ohio	1958–1981
Byron R. White	Colorado	1962–1993
Arthur J. Goldberg	Illinois	1962–1965
Abe Fortas	Tennessee	1965–1969
Thurgood Marshall	New York	1967–1991
Harry A. Blackmun	Minnesota	1970–1994
Lewis F. Powell, Jr.	Virginia	1972–1987
William H. Rehnquist*	Arizona	1972–1986
John Paul Stevens	Illinois	1975–
Sandra Day O'Connor	Arizona	1981–
Antonin Scalia	District of Columbia	1986–
Anthony M. Kennedy	California	1988–
David H. Souter	New Hampshire	1990–
Clarence Thomas	District of Columbia	1991–
Ruth Bader Ginsburg	District of Columbia	1993–
Stephen G. Breyer	Massachusetts	1994–

*Served as both chief justice and associate justice.

Answers to "Fact Checkers"

Chapter 1

Across

2. articles
3. limited
5. divine
6. people
7. preamble

Down

1. judicial
2. amendments
4. consent

Chapter 2

Right: freedom of speech, freedom of religion, voting

Responsibility: obeying the law, serving on a jury, paying taxes

Requirement: ability to speak English, belief in democracy, sense of morality

Chapter 3

1. candidates
2. campaigns
3. parties
4. primary
5. delegates
6. convention
7. mate
8. general
9. electors
10. electoral
11. popular

Chapter 4

Legislative powers: make tax laws, make immigration laws

Nonlegislative powers: impeach a government leader, regulate interstate commerce, propose constitutional amendments, break ties in the electoral college

Implied powers: investigative powers, legislative oversight

Denied powers: suspend writ of habeas corpus, make ex post facto laws, convict a person without a trial

Chapter 5

1. federal
2. defendant
3. civil
4. defendant
5. jury
6. appellate

Chapter 6

1. pardon
2. impeached
3. press
4. cabinet
5. veto
6. two
7. treaties
8. implied
9. weapons
10. fourteen
11. Senate

Chapter 7

Across

2. president
5. domestic
7. aid
8. security
9. foreign

Down

1. Medicare
3. trade
4. regulation
6. treaties

Chapter 8

1. e
2. a
3. f
4. b
5. g
6. h
7. d
8. c

Chapter 9

1. governor
2. lieutenant
3. mansion
4. state
5. judges
6. bicameral
7. four

Chapter 10

national defense

maintenance of national parklands

creation of foreign policy

establishment of post offices

Chapter 11

1. Great Britain, Japan, France
2. China
3. Great Britain
4. China
5. Japan
6. China
7. China
8. Great Britain, France, Japan
9. France
10. Japan, Great Britain
11. France
12. Japan

INDEX

federal government:
  budget of, 93
  executive branch of, 64–73
  judicial branch of, 52–59
  legislative branch of, 38–47
  origins of, 8–9
  policy set by, 81
  powers of, 10, 101, 106
  strength of, 29, 34
  taxation by, 91–92
federalism, 9
Federalist Party, 8, 29
filibuster, 46
Five Nations, 8
foreign aid, 83
foreign policy, 67, 81, 83, 84, 85, 91
foreign relations, 44
framers, 8, 9, 10, 43, 47, 55, 91
freedom of assembly, 20
freedom of religion, 20
freedom of speech, 20
freedom of the press, 21
Free Soil Party, 30
French government, 120, 124–125

general election, 28, 32, 33
George III (king of England), 7
Gideon v. Wainwright, 59
Gore, Al, 30, 33, 69
governor, 99, 101–103
grand jury, 56, 57
Great Council, 5
green card, 19
Green Party, 30

habeus corpus, 45
Hamilton, Alexander, 29
head of state, 68, 72
health, 82, 83
Health and Human Services, Department of, 70
health and human services, secretary of, 70
House of Commons, 5, 41, 123, 124
House of Lords, 5, 41, 123, 124
House of Representatives:
  bills passed in, 46–47, 69
  elections for, 33
  leadership of, 43

in legislative branch, 9, 41
  organization of, 39
  in political process, 29
House of Representatives (*Cont.*):
  powers of, 44–45
  representation in, 42–43
housing, 82, 83
Housing and Urban Development, Department of, 70
housing and urban development, secretary of, 70
human rights, 84

immigrant, 17, 19, 22
immigration, 44
Immigration and Naturalization Service, 17, 19, 22
impeachment, 3, 45, 69
implied powers, 44, 45, 47
independence, 6, 7
independent voters, 30
integration, 10
interest group, 33, 46, 116
Interior, Department of the, 70
interior, secretary of the, 70
Internal Revenue Service, 91
interstate commerce, 44
investigative powers, 45
Iroquois Confederation of the Five Nations, 8

Jackson, Andrew, 29
Jamestown, 6
Japanese government, 121, 125–126
Jefferson, Thomas, 7, 8, 29, 45
John (king of England), 6
Johnson, Andrew, 69
Johnson, Lyndon, 85
judges, federal, 3, 17, 20, 45, 55, 57, 58, 59, 104
judges, state, 104, 106
judicial branch, state, 99, 103–104
judicial branch, U.S., 3, 9, 10, 52–59, 120
judicial review, 9, 58
juries, 21, 22, 56, 57
jurisdiction, 55
Justice, Department of, 70

Labor, Department of, 70
labor, secretary of, 70